JOY OUT of SORROW

A Birth Mother's Journey of Healing through His Mercy

TRACY DUNN LYONS

WESTBOW
PRESS®
A DIVISION OF THOMAS NELSON
& ZONDERVAN

Copyright © 2022 Tracy Dunn Lyons.

All rights reserved. No part of this book may be used or reproduced by any means, graphic, electronic, or mechanical, including photocopying, recording, taping or by any information storage retrieval system without the written permission of the author except in the case of brief quotations embodied in critical articles and reviews.

This book is a work of non-fiction. Unless otherwise noted, the author and the publisher make no explicit guarantees as to the accuracy of the information contained in this book and in some cases, names of people and places have been altered to protect their privacy.

WestBow Press books may be ordered through booksellers or by contacting:

WestBow Press
A Division of Thomas Nelson & Zondervan
1663 Liberty Drive
Bloomington, IN 47403
www.westbowpress.com
844-714-3454

Because of the dynamic nature of the Internet, any web addresses or links contained in this book may have changed since publication and may no longer be valid. The views expressed in this work are solely those of the author and do not necessarily reflect the views of the publisher, and the publisher hereby disclaims any responsibility for them.

Any people depicted in stock imagery provided by Getty Images are models, and such images are being used for illustrative purposes only. Certain stock imagery © Getty Images.

Scripture quotations are from Revised Standard Version of the Bible—Second Catholic Edition (Ignatius Edition) Copyright © 2006 National Council of the Churches of Christ in the United States of America. Used by permission. All rights reserved worldwide.

ISBN: 978-1-6642-8089-2 (sc)
ISBN: 978-1-6642-8090-8 (hc)
ISBN: 978-1-6642-8088-5 (e)

Library of Congress Control Number: 2022919048

Print information available on the last page.

WestBow Press rev. date: 10/28/2022

*Dedicated to Tammy,
my angel in heaven.*

CHAPTER 1

It felt like the longest two minutes of my life. I guess it was two minutes; it's kind of a blur now. Waiting for the little, white-and-purple stick to tell me my fate was painful. I kind of already knew, strange as it sounds. I had been scared this would happen. I knew we weren't careful. I won't get into the messy details, but I wasn't persistent enough about being careful. In those two short minutes, my mind went from fear to sadness to confusion. I was afraid for so many things. Afraid for it to be positive. Afraid for what it would mean. The anticipation was almost too much to handle. I knew in my gut what the little stick on the back of the toilet was going to say before I saw it. Two lines. Yep. Two pink lines.

I was pregnant.

What in the world was I going to do? I was seventeen and a senior in high school. I was going to graduate in about four weeks. I was in a relationship that I knew wasn't good for me, yet I couldn't get out of it. Those two pink lines sure seemed to complicate things so much. My perfect from the outside world had just been flipped upside down. I wasn't sure where to turn. For a few weeks, no one knew except the father and me. I knew it couldn't stay a secret forever, but I just wasn't ready to face it, or my family.

I was born in 1980 in a small town in Louisiana called Alexandria. I was the second of two children, with a brother fifteen months older than me. My parents were both from large families with many siblings. My dad was the second of ten children and was brought up in a very religious home. Our home was very similar. We went to Mass every Sunday and prayed at night before bed. I knew God existed, but I did not have a one-on-one relationship with him.

Much was expected of me as a child. I was very bright and did well in school, which led to expectations of perfection. I'm honestly not sure if the expectations were greater from my father or from myself. I felt like the way to make my parents proud of me was to do well in school and stay out of trouble. I followed the rules and had good friends who stayed out of trouble as well. I always wanted to make everyone happy and make sure no one was ever angry with me. What others thought of me was always so important to me—too important. I think my parents just assumed that I would always do the right thing so there was never talk about what to do in certain situations that came about as I got older.

In high school, the temptations were greater to veer from the right path. Those temptations seemed so much more exciting and appealing than my straight and narrow path of being good. What could one drink at a party hurt? I would still be able to keep my grades up, and all my friends were doing it. So where was the harm? What I didn't know was that those things would cause me to lose my inhibitions and send me down a path that would change my life forever.

When the friend of an old boyfriend started calling me, it was exciting. I felt like I was being pursued. No one had ever really done that before, and it was fun. We talked on the phone for weeks before going on an official date. I felt like I could talk to him about anything. When we finally did go on a date, we went bowling and then hung out at his house where no one was home. This should have been my first clue, but I was enjoying being in the moment so I didn't mind. Things almost went too far that night, but I stopped him. I don't think he said anything negative about it that night, but I remember feeling like I had let him down. I was so wrapped up in the moment and the rush of the relationship that I did not even think about what the right thing to do was. I wasn't armed with anything. Like I said before, I think my parents always thought I would do the right thing so there was no discussion of situations like this. I liked the fact that someone was paying attention to me, so the relationship progressed to the point where we were staring at the stick on the back of the toilet. We had been dating for several months at this point, and it was nearing the end of my senior year of high school.

Our relationship was never perfect. It was up and down. I ignored the fact that he may have been seeing other people because I wanted him to like me so much. I was so insecure in being alone that I stayed in a relationship that wasn't much of a relationship. I wasn't happy but just couldn't get out of it. My parents weren't too fond of him; they could see he wasn't good for me. I just ignored their words of warning.

The reality of having to tell my parents and family was terrifying. I knew telling them would be one of the hardest things to do, so I just didn't. I was afraid of letting them down. I kept it secret from almost everyone. I think I was just trying to figure out what I was going to do with the information and how I was going to face it. And maybe if I didn't say it out loud, it wouldn't be real. We told the father's parents, who suggested I have an abortion. I didn't know what to do, but I knew I didn't want to do that. I was shocked at how quickly that was suggested. My family was very Catholic and had instilled strong values in me about the importance of life. My grandmother had a bumper sticker on her car that said, "It's a child, not a choice." I loved that sticker. I knew that abortion was not something I would ever be willing to do.

I think the suggestion of an abortion was when my eyes began to open about the toxicity of our relationship and our values not being in alignment. I was even more confused now. There was a small part of me that wanted this to change him, to change us, but the more this pregnancy became a reality, the more I knew that wasn't the case. I went on about my days going to school and pretending that everything was perfectly normal when they were anything but that. On the inside I was a nervous wreck, knowing my world was changing.

A few weeks later, I got really sick. I couldn't hold anything down and became very weak. I knew what was wrong but still couldn't get the words out. My parents assumed I had a stomach virus and made an appointment with the doctor. I got dressed and rode with my mom to the doctor. I knew what was going to happen here. My stomach hurt even more as we walked into the exam room and sat down. The doctor asked me when the date of my last period was. When I said it, I'll never forget he put his pen down and looked at me. I'm sure all the blood rushed out of my face. I was scared to hear what he would say. He asked, "Is there any way you could be pregnant?" Knowing that I already was, I said, "I guess so. I don't know." I felt the air suck out of the room. My stomach did flip flops and I just wanted to crawl under the table. My mom put her head down and didn't look up. The doctor turned and walked out. My mother stayed silent. I waited for her to look at me or say something, but no. Silence. I was dying for her to say something, anything, to me. Yell, scream, cry—something to acknowledge that this was happening. I needed by mom in that moment, even an angry mom, but I got nothing. I felt even more alone.

Shortly thereafter, the nurse returned to draw some blood. You could've heard a pin drop; no one said a word. The next few minutes were long and silent. The doctor came back in and said, "Well, you're pregnant." I didn't know how to respond. Tears rolled down my face at hearing the news that I already knew. It was hard to hear out loud. I felt so guilty. This wasn't the way I should've told my parents, but I was relieved to have someone else do it for me. My mom stayed silent and didn't even look at me. I know she was hurt. I was hurting too, and confused and upset. I wished she would just talk to me.

We left the doctor's office shortly after hearing the news; my mom couldn't get to the car fast enough. She didn't say a word on the drive home, and then when we walked in the door, she told me to call my dad and tell him. This was long before texting and cell phones so we couldn't call him from the car. I sat down on our old, brown couch in the living room and called my dad at work. I was so nervous that he was going to react the same way my mom had. He had always been the stricter one when it came to discipline. I knew I had messed up, but I really needed someone to be on my side in that moment. I didn't think it would be him, which made me even more scared to tell him. My voice was shaking as I told him the news that I was pregnant. There was a short pause and then he told me that he loved me and that everything would be OK. I couldn't stop crying. This was not the reaction I expected from my dad. I expected yelling and chastisement. I expected the worst. Looking back now, I see this was God loving me through my dad. I had fallen and made a mistake, and he loved me anyway. I needed that love so much that day and was so relieved.

The father was not present for any of this. We had not discussed how to tell my parents, or really anything of significance. I had already started distancing myself from him. This pregnancy, this child, had opened my eyes to the direction we were going. It was a toxic relationship, and I hadn't seen it. I was so blinded by wanting to be loved and valued that I couldn't see what was really happening. I put my whole worth in whether he liked me. I was very codependent and felt I needed to be in a relationship to feel worthy. He didn't really value me, and I honestly didn't really value him. I knew that this wasn't a relationship that I would want to be an example of love to my child. I wanted better for him or her. I told him I wanted to break up a few days after the doctor's appointment. He wasn't happy about it but couldn't stop me. For probably the first time, I put my thoughts and feelings above someone else's and did what was right for me. It wasn't easy. I would have preferred not to be alone, but I just needed more than he could give me. I felt relieved but scared. What was I going to do now?

CHAPTER 2

Instead of focusing on the last few weeks of high school and having fun with my friends, I was having to frantically change course. I had planned to go to LSU with all my friends the next year. Well, that wasn't going to happen. I was so sad. I knew changes had to me made, but I didn't have to like them. I quickly applied for a scholarship at a local college and decided to spend my first year of college at home. For years I had planned to get out of this town and here I was having to stay. I had no one to blame by myself, but it didn't make it any more fun. I wasn't excited anymore about graduation or any of the end of the year activities. They all felt like things I had to get through now, especially senior prom.

Isn't senior prom supposed to be one of the best nights in a high school person's life? Prom should be the fun ending to a chapter of youth. Well, my youth had officially ended several weeks prior so this night was not a dream come true. I did not want to go. I certainly did not want to go with the baby's father. We had broken up a week or so before, but he'd already rented a tux so I felt bad and off we went. I wasn't excited at all. I didn't look pregnant at all, but I couldn't help but worry that someone would figure me out. I made sure my dress was loose in the front just in case. We met at a friend's house to ride together in a limo. I knew that we would be stopping at a daiquiri shop and one of the moms was planning to buy everyone drinks. Only a handful of my close friends knew about my pregnancy at the time, and I wasn't ready for word to get out yet so I begged my mom to meet us at the daiquiri shop. She bought me one without alcohol in it, a virgin daiquiri. When she brought it to me in the car, on the side of the stark white Styrofoam cup was written in black marker, "Virgin." That was a slap in the face, if only everyone could see the irony in that right. My friend said to just put my hand over it when I held it so that no one could see the writing. I don't know if anyone noticed, but I was embarrassed anyway. I sank down in my seat and sulked. It was about more than a drink. It was just another way that my life had changed. I couldn't be the carefree teenager anymore. I wanted so badly to wish it away. As horrible as it sounds, I just wanted to wake up and it all would be a bad dream. But that wasn't reality. I didn't want to accept it.

The dance was fairly uneventful. I didn't dance much, just sat at the table with him while feeling sorry for myself. I did not want to dance with him. We had already broken up and I didn't want anything to do with him. So instead of just hanging with my friends, I sat at the table miserable.

After the dance, we went to the school cafeteria for breakfast. I guess he had gotten tired of me pouting and avoiding him and he got mad. He said some things, yelled, pushed a bench, and pretty much made a scene. It was embarrassing. Everyone was staring. I was so mad at him for making a scene, but deep down I was mad at him for so much more, and at myself. I just wanted to get out of there and away from him.

I took him home and when we got to his house, he wouldn't get out of my car. He said some things, I said some things, and I was done. I was done with his controlling me, done with my inability to be alone, done with needing approval from someone else, just done. This pregnancy had woken me up to the fact that we were not good for each other and I wanted better for my child and myself.

Eventually, after an hour of asking him to get out, he did. That would be the last time I would see or talk to him for months. I drove back home crying, ashamed, and alone. Was I really going to do this by myself? Was I strong enough? I wondered if I should get back together with him just to have someone to go through this with. I knew this wasn't the answer, but I didn't know what was. I prayed that night on the way home, but not in a way that I am proud of. I wanted so badly for all this to not be really happening so I prayed for God to end it. I didn't want to have an abortion, but I didn't want to be pregnant either. I didn't have the support of a loving partner, and I didn't have the support from my family. I felt so alone. I asked God to take it away from me. I'm not proud of these prayers. They make me feel guilty and selfish to this day. Thankfully God answered my prayer in another way, but in that time, I felt he didn't hear me, and I was abandoned by him too.

Graduation was the next event I had to make it through, which meant finishing up classes and taking finals. I felt like I was doing a good job of pretending to still be the perfect child and student. Few people knew my secret and I intended to keep it that way, at least from the teachers and staff. Until one day in class, I got hot and nauseated. I felt like I was going to pass out. My friends got me a cold rag and some water while my teacher, who was concerned, was giving me that look. You know the look. The look you give someone when you know they are hiding something and you think you know what it is. I can still see the look she gave me. I know she knew or at least suspected. I'm sure my look back said, "Please don't tell anyone" or "I'm so scared." I just knew that if she said something, I would not be able to deny it. Having a few people know that I wasn't perfect was hard enough, but if it had gotten out to the whole school before I graduated, I would have been devastated. She didn't say anything to me or to anyone. My secret was kept for a little longer.

Graduation is something a teenager looks forward to for four years, a milestone to be celebrated. It didn't feel much like a celebration to me. My mom's family was coming to go to graduation, and she asked that we not tell anyone about the pregnancy yet. I wasn't surprised by her request, but a little hurt. I was already embarrassed and guilty enough, now to be asked to continue to hide it from my family made it worse. I was an embarrassment. I'm not very good as keeping secrets or hiding my feelings, so I just avoided them as much as possible. I just wanted it to be over with so we could move into the next chapter, whatever that was going to be.

So many things took place over the next few months of summer. Instead of going on trips and goofing off all summer, I got a job at a local ice cream shop to start saving money for this baby I was caring. Adulthood came really fast. Everything was going to be so expensive. I couldn't imagine my parents helping much, so I needed to fend for myself. The things we take for granted as children come quickly into focus when faced with adult life challenges, insurance being one. I had taken for granted that my parents' insurance would cover my expenses, but that was not the case. We did not have maternity coverage on our insurance, so I was forced to apply for Medicaid.

I drive past that building often. It is no longer a Medicaid office. I think it is a Realtor office now, but I think of that day every time I drive by. After discovering that I needed other insurance coverage, my mom made me apply for Medicaid. Yet another embarrassing moment for me. I did not grow up rich by any means, but we weren't poor either. Wasn't Medicaid for poor people? I could not understand why I had to do this. After filling out all the forms I needed, my mom sent me there by myself, with the letter. In the letter, she had written how she and my dad would not support my pregnancy and therefore I needed financial assistance. I knew deep down that this was to get my medical expenses covered, but man did those words sting. The truth was that they were true. My mom was still not really talking to me and definitely wasn't talking to me about the pregnancy. So while the letter was referring to financial support, the lack of emotional support hurt much worse.

I sat in the cold, bright office with many other people for what seemed like hours, waiting for my name to be called. When my turn finally came, I handed them my papers and watched as the person read all of them. She asked if I was applying for WIC as well, and I said I guess so. She told me this would give me money for food while I was pregnant and then formula for after the baby was born. I was approved for all of it and started getting the vouchers for food. My mom would take me to the store late at night so that no one would see us using government assistance to get the food, heaven forbid anyone think we weren't perfect. I know lots of people use this and I don't mean to be derogatory about it, but at that point in my life, it was one more thing to be embarrassed about. I felt so much guilt and shame for all of this and this was just one more thing to add to my guilt. I hated every second of it.

As I neared the halfway mark of my pregnancy, I began school at the local Baptist college. I could no longer hide my growing belly, and the whispers and stares started. I definitely stood out like a sore thumb at school, which made it difficult to make new friends. I basically went to school, work, and home. My friends had all moved away so my support system was gone. My dad was semi supportive in that he would often ask how I was feeling or if I needed anything, but my mom acted like all was normal. She still had not told her mom or sisters. I guess she felt like if we didn't talk about it, it wouldn't happen. I needed someone to talk about it with but had to bottle all my feelings up and pretend like it wasn't happening.

The day finally arrived when I would have an ultrasound. I was wearing white shorts overalls and a blue shirt. Overalls were my go-to outfit because I could hide my belly while wearing them. My mom had decided to come with me to this appointment. She and I went alone. I hadn't talked to the father in months, so I didn't tell him about it. I was just glad my mom was there that day; a little support was better than no support.

They called my name and we went back to the ultrasound room. I don't know why I was so nervous. I guess the ultrasound and knowing the sex of the baby would make it real. I don't think anything can prepare you for the emotions of seeing a human growing inside you on the screen for the first time. It was a real baby with a head, hands, feet, and a strong heart. She said, "It's a boy." I was overcome with love for this unborn baby boy growing in me. I was glad my mom had decided to come. I think seeing him softened her heart a bit that day. She didn't say much, but I could feel her coming around.

He was perfect. Seeing him for the first time both excited and terrified me at the same time. He looked so sweet and innocent. I wondered how in the world I was going to keep him safe. What was I going to do with this beautiful baby boy? I think that was the day God began to work on my heart to see that maybe his plan was bigger than I ever could imagine. Maybe there was something different in store for our lives and our journey. I didn't know then, but his future had already been determined and prepared for.

> For I know that plans I have for you, says the Lord, plans for welfare and not for evil, to give you a future and a hope. (Jeremiah 29:11)

CHAPTER

3

I N EARLY FALL 1998, I WAS AT HOME IN THE MIDDLE OF THE DAY, resting between classes, when the home phone rang. I was lying on the couch in my parents' living room. My stomach was starting to get bigger, so jumping up to run to the phone wasn't easy. I was a little out of breath when I answered, and it was one of my aunts on the other end of the line.

I come from a very large family, my dad being the second oldest of ten. Some of his siblings were not too much older than me and felt more like my siblings at times. Most of them had not been very supportive so far, with some of them blatantly ignoring me when I was around, so I was surprised by her call. She asked me about school, how I was feeling, and about the pregnancy. The small talk felt awkward given the lack of support I had felt so far. Then she asked me a question that I don't think I will ever forget. She asked me why I wanted to keep the baby. Silence. I didn't have an answer. I said, "Because he is my baby." I didn't really know what else to say. I couldn't say, "Because I love the father and we are starting a family." That wasn't true. I couldn't say, "Because I'm prepared and have lots of people who support me," because I wasn't, and I didn't. She asked me if I'd ever thought about placing my baby for adoption. Of course, I had not. I had not really thought of anything but the present moment. I knew that I had chosen life when I chose not to have an abortion, but I honestly had not thought of any other choice I could make besides keeping the baby. She then suggested I attend a support group she had found for me for pregnant teens. Reluctantly, I agreed. I don't know why I agreed. Maybe I was being obedient to an adult. Maybe something felt right, but I agreed and went.

The first day I walked into the Volunteers of America (VOA), I was terrified. Here I was, scared, alone, and walking into an unfamiliar place to have a group meeting with people I didn't know. No one came with me to this meeting. I went alone, without a friend or family, just me and my fear of the unknown. Those who know me know that I am very shy and don't make friends easily, so I was very intimidated. When I pulled up in the parking lot, I almost didn't go in. My nerves almost got the best of me, but I went inside anyway. The VOA felt like an office building. It wasn't very warm and inviting, but I was met with smiling, warm faces. The first person to greet me was a counselor. She welcomed me and showed me to the room where the group meeting would take place.

I was brought into a room with several other girls who were obviously pregnant and several who weren't. We went around the table and introduced ourselves, and each told a little bit about our story. I was so nervous. I told them my name and when I was due, and that was it. I'm pretty sure I could hear my heart beating over my words. I was just hoping the other girls didn't notice how nervous I was. I kept my head down while the others spoke about themselves, but my interest was sparked when the nonpregnant girls started talking. One of them had kept her baby and was there to tell us about being a teen mom. She talked about how hard it was and how daily life was a struggle. She talked about the joys of motherhood as well, but all I could think about was how tough it must be for her. I put myself in her shoes and saw many hard days ahead. Trying to go to school, work, and take care of a baby would be difficult with the lack of support I had.

The other girl talked about placing her baby for an open adoption. I had never heard of this before. I always thought you had the baby and it was immediately taken away, that you would never see them or hold them. She had a much different story. She talked about picking out the parents for her baby and meeting them before the baby was born. She talked about how she still got to see her every once in a while. When I put myself in this girl's shoes, it didn't seem as scary as I thought. It seemed kind of beautiful. I didn't see any of those girls again. I didn't know any of them. I don't know which path they chose or if that meeting meant as much to them as it did to me. God tugged on my heart at that meeting and planted a seed of hope in me that left me wanting to go back there and hear more.

Over the next few weeks, I went to the VOA and met with my counselor a couple of times a week. We would talk about pregnancy and how I was feeling and explore options for me. Through our meetings, I discovered that I had a pattern of very unhealthy relationships based on codependency; I needed a person to affirm me and to make me feel loved. This was why I found myself in relationships where I did everything I could to please the other person, even things I shouldn't. She and I had long talks about what life would look like if I kept the baby. We talked about the lack of support from my family, my absent relationship with the father, and how all my close friends had moved away. The more we talked, the more God nudged me to explore adoption. I knew that I loved this baby boy so much and wanted the best for him, even if that didn't include me. Even though I knew that keeping him would give me someone who would love and accept me no matter what, his happiness became more important than my own. It was now my job to make sure he grew up in the best family with the support he deserved. I watched videos and read every book on adoption that I could get my hands on. I was struggling with my guilt and shame of disappointing my parents and knew this might be a decision they would support. I still wasn't completely sure, but I knew it was something I needed to look into.

While sitting at the dinner table one night, I decided to tell my parents my decision. I told them about all the meetings I had had with my counselor and all about the support group I had been to. I told them I was thinking adoption may be best for my baby and asked what they thought of it. They both sat in silence for a minute before getting teary. They both agreed that as hard as it would be, this was probably the best decision and they would support me in any way I needed. From that day on, things changed in my house. I think their feelings went from embarrassment to pride. More conversations were had about adoption, pregnancy, and just how I was doing in general. It was as if a switch had been flipped and they were both on my side. That felt so good. I had needed this support for so long and was so glad they were both being there for me.

    I talked with my counselor and came up with a list of parent must-haves so I could start a search for the perfect parents for my precious baby. The list included several key things. They must be Catholic, they must want to send their children to Catholic school, they must be open to an open adoption, and they must want to meet with me several times a year after he was born. My counselor looked at my list and knew it would be tough to find people who met all these standards. Looking back now, I probably was really giving that list to God and testing him to see if this was the right thing. I think maybe part of me wanted to not be able to find parents who would fulfill the list because then I would just keep him. I had a constant inner battle with myself about this decision. Most days it felt like the right thing to do, but some days were just hard. I wasn't quite sure I was strong enough to handle it.

    My counselor gathered for me many "Dear Birth Mother" letters to look at from different adoption agencies all over the state. "Dear Birth Mother" letters are letters prospective adoptive parents write to give a little information about themselves and the types of adoption they are open to. My parents and I sat at their kitchen table and read every one over and over. I was so overwhelmed. How would I pick the perfect parents for my child? I was unsure. I immediately pulled out all the ones who did not want an open adoption or contact after the birth. My love for this baby was so strong. I knew that not seeing him ever again was not an option. There really weren't many families who met my criteria, so I had to widen my range. My dad picked up one of the papers I had set to the side and asked me to read it again. They sounded great, except they only wanted to communicate with letters and pictures after the birth. I wasn't sure that would be enough for me, but something told me to keep them in the maybe pile. After days of reading the letters over and over, I finally narrowed it down to three families and decided to get more information about them to see if I wanted to meet them.

The next step in the process was to get scrapbook albums from each family. The families had put together pictures of themselves and their families with more information about them. One of the couples looked like a nice family. They were both nurses. I loved that because I wanted to work in the medical field too. They lived in Louisiana, about two hours from where I did. They were both Catholic and wanted to send their children to Catholic school. They seemed perfect on paper. This was the family my dad had asked me to read the letter again. The only negative I found in them was the lack of contact after the birth. I decided to set up a meeting with them to check them out anyway. We set up a meeting for the week of Thanksgiving where my parents and I would meet them.

CHAPTER

4

*N*ERVOUS IS NOT A DESCRIPTIVE ENOUGH WORD TO EXPLAIN how I felt that November day. Here I was, eight months pregnant at eighteen years old, about to meet the people who may be the future parents of my child. I could not get my thoughts and emotions in check. I was excited, scared, nervous, tearful, and hopeful all at the same time. What if they were awful? What if they weren't the right fit? What if they didn't like me? What if they would never let me see him again if I gave him to them? All these questions were swirling around in my head. My parents and I had arrived at the VOA a few minutes early to get settled and ready for this visit. I don't know if I ever could really have been ready for what was to come.

I was sitting in a chair facing the door when they walked in. I've tried to come up with the words to explain the feelings I had in that moment, and I just can't. I could maybe relate it to the moment when the infant leaped in the womb of Elizabeth as she greeted Mary. Something, or someone, inside me just knew. It was them. I hadn't even spoken one word to them yet and I knew it was them. They were perfect for him.

Her name was Tammy, and his was Rickie. They were young, early thirties, and I could see the excitement in their eyes as they walked in. We hugged and she sat next to me and her husband next to her. I couldn't take my eyes off them. We talked for a while. I asked questions about them, and they asked questions about me. By the end of the meeting, it was as if we were old friends. I asked if they wanted to return a few days later and go to the doctor with me to hear the heartbeat, and they happily agreed.

When we started to say our goodbyes, Tammy took her necklace off and handed it to me. She had been wearing a cross and a St. Gerard medal since starting the adoption process, praying for the future mother of her child, and she wanted me to have it. All I could do was cry. God had given me a good Catholic couple who had truly prayed for this moment. I am certain that her prayers had gotten me through the last few months and had gotten us to this moment. He had fulfilled my checklist and so much more. We exchanged phone numbers, and I said I would keep in touch with doctor's appointments.

I did not meet with any other couples; I didn't need to. I knew that my baby would have a loving home with this family and that was really all that mattered. We never talked about visits or communication for after the birth. I just didn't worry about it anymore. I knew deep down that God had it covered. I don't know if you can ever be 100 percent sure about a decision like this, but I knew something felt right about it. I spent a lot of time over the few days and weeks after that first meeting wondering what his life would be like with them. I felt comforted knowing it would be good.

The next week, they met me for my doctor's appointment. I could see the nervous excitement on their faces. I could also see the apprehension on the faces of the doctor and nurses. I'm sure this is not something they dealt with often. I explained to my doctor and the nurse that I had decided to place my baby for adoption and that these would be his parents. I think this was the first time I had said it out loud. It felt right. I knew in my heart that this was the right thing for all of us, but I don't think I truly understood how deeply this decision would affect the rest of my life and change me.

Up until this point, I had not seen the father since the night of my senior prom. I called him to tell him that the baby was a boy but had to leave a message with his mom, and I never heard back from him. When I made the decision about adoption, I decided it was time to see him again. I called and told him we needed to talk and needed to do it face-to-face. I was not nervous to tell him; I don't know why. I think by that point I was firm in my decision and didn't feel like I needed his approval. Maybe that was wrong. Maybe I should have included him more in that process, but this wasn't about us anymore; it was about the best interests of our baby. I told him about my decision for adoption and that I had picked and met with the parents. He didn't take it so well. He was not happy with this and made sure I knew it. He stormed out and once again disappeared. I didn't see or hear from him again until the day I delivered. I trusted God would work out whatever needed to happen though and didn't dwell too much on it.

Over the next few weeks, life went on as normal as it could. I finished up finals for my first semester at college. I could hardly fit in the desks anymore and people were definitely starting to stare more. Being eighteen, pregnant, and going to a Baptist college made for lots of looks and whispers. As much as I tried to ignore them, I was more and more embarrassed by my growing belly. I went straight to class and straight home every day to avoid conversation. I think at the time I assumed people were avoiding me, but the truth was that I was avoiding them and any questions that would come. When anyone would happen to ask if I was ready or excited, I wouldn't know what to say. I couldn't very well tell a stranger that I wasn't ready and I wasn't excited. I couldn't tell them all my fears about adoption and my worry whether this was the right decision. To avoid this, I just stayed home most of the time.

The end of the semester and winter break also meant that my friends who were away at college would be coming home. I had a great core group of friends who supported me no matter what, and I couldn't wait to have them around again. They had been checking on me often and knew and supported my decision for adoption. One of them even went to a birthing class with me and was going to be my delivery coach. I shared my fears about the future with them and we cried and laughed together. The night before I was to go in to be induced, they all came to spend the night to be with me at my parents' house. My counselor had let the father know that the next day would be the day and that he would be able to see the baby. I did not want him in the delivery room but wouldn't keep him from seeing the baby after. I couldn't sleep out of nervous excitement, and they stayed up with me to calm me down. I don't know if I could have gotten through the next few days without them. I did not know how dark they would really be.

> For this child I prayed; and the Lord has granted me
> my petition which I made to him. (1 Samuel 1:27)

CHAPTER

5

On December 22, 1998, the alarm went off at 4 a.m. I'm not sure it really woke me up; I'm not sure I slept at all. I tossed and turned all night long, thinking and worrying about what the day would bring. Would it bring joy, happiness, and peace, or would it be too sad to bear? I had to face it head-on, and I had to be there by five so I had to get a move on. I got up and got dressed like it was any other day, knowing that it wasn't just any other day. My mom and I set out for the hospital before anyone else got up to get checked in. My friends stayed back at my house to sleep in a little; no use in everyone getting up so early. I needed them well rested for my support later. We arrived at the hospital and checked in, and they sent us to a room to get prepped for the day.

Prepped? Ha! That's the word they had used the day before when they told me what time to be there. I'm not sure in my eighteen-year-old world I was ready for their "prep." There were tubes, needles, bags, razors, and talk of an enema. I thought, *You want to put what where? I don't think so.* But I went through the motions and did what I was told, no matter how strange it was to me. When they deemed me "ready," they started the medication Pitocin to induce my labor.

Here we go. *Ready* seemed like such a strange word for that day and that moment. Physically, I was ready. I mean, my goodness, I looked like I had swallowed a giant beach ball. Not the cute little beach balls kids play with in the pool and at the beach. No, the giant ones they throw around at concerts and sporting events, the really big ones. Physically it was time, but was I ready emotionally? No. I knew going into that day that emotions would be high, but I honestly had no Idea. I don't think anyone is ever truly ready emotionally for what happens when you give birth. I definitely wasn't ready for the extra emotions involved in adoption. I was naïve in thinking I was ready and could handle it.

The contractions began shortly after the medication was started. They weren't too bad at first. I had plenty of distractions. My friends and some of my family had arrived to keep me company. They all thought it was fun to tell me when the contractions would start and end based on the monitor readings, as if I didn't know from the feeling of my insides being squeezed by a vice. My close group of four friends stayed with me most of the day, as did my mom and my grandmother. It felt good to have everyone there supporting me, especially my mom and grandmother. They really surprised me in how they never left my side all day. I was so relieved to not have to worry about support that day. I had been worried they would not be there for me, but I was wrong. I felt so much love from them at the exact moment I needed it most. My dad, brother, other friends, and some relatives were in and out often. They were able to keep my mind off what was really happening for a while.

The doctor finally came in and decided it was time to break my water, yet another thing no one can prepare you for. After about five hundred gallons of fluid had come out, things got real. The pain after that was like nothing I could ever describe. Each contraction now made me angry. The usual things people say to women hurting in labor couldn't be said to me, such as "It'll be worth it in the end," "All the pain will be a memory when you hold the baby," and other words that were not appropriate. I began to resent these pains. They reminded me not of the life I was giving birth to but of the loss I was about to experience. I wanted all of this to go away, to skip this part. Unfortunately, this was not possible, and I would have to endure this pain.

Just like that, the mood in the room changed. I was hurting, angry, and sad. I was not nice. People began to filter out of the room to give me some space. I don't blame them; I wouldn't have wanted to be around me either. Despite anything I said or how much I was hurting, my mom, close friends, and grandmother never left my side. They were definitely my rocks that day, and I know God sent each of them to me that day to lift me up. I honestly don't think I would have made it that day or the days that followed without their love and support.

After several hours of awful pain, I finally got an epidural. Relief! I didn't feel anything. I was numb physically, and I think emotionally too because now I just wanted to sleep. I kicked everyone out of the room except for my best friend, and we took naps. I welcomed sleep for a little while to escape the reality of what would soon occur.

The nap didn't last too long before it was time. It was time for him to arrive, time for me to face this head-on, and time for me to be strong. Two hours of pushing something I couldn't feel was definitely hard work. I didn't think I would ever be able to deliver him. It felt like we were getting nowhere, and I was exhausted. The doctor began to get concerned that we would have to resort to surgery, but finally the baby decided he would relent and come out.

I got a quick glimpse of him as the doctor was cleaning him up, and he was perfect. I know all moms say that about their babies, but really, he was perfect. At nine pounds and eight ounces, he had no room for wrinkled-up skin or features you typically see in a newborn. He looked like a one-month-old. The doctor quickly handed him over to the nurses, who brought him to the warmer to check on him. I was confused. Don't moms usually hold their babies right away? Why wouldn't they give him to me? I looked from the area where he was and back to the doctor with a scared and confused look on my face. Maybe they thought I didn't want to hold him because of the adoption. Maybe that was the only look I would get of him at all. In those few short minutes, a thousand worries flew through my mind, until finally the nurse came to ask me if I wanted to hold him. They had verified with me that I would want to hold him several times throughout the day, and I had said yes every time so I was aggravated that they were asking again. I replied, "Yes, please bring him to me." Reluctantly, she went to get him.

Tears rolled down my cheeks as she placed him in my arms. I could not believe that this precious gift from God was finally here and in my arms. I had never known such instant love as I did in that very moment. I'm not sure what anyone else in that room was doing at the moment, because all I could see was this perfect baby boy. All the worry, stress, and fear that I had been experiencing over the past few weeks seemed to disappear in that moment. Nothing else mattered except this perfect gift from above. The warmth of his body next to mine was all the comfort I needed. I held him tight and just stared at his perfect little face. Time seemed to stand still, and I was willing to let it. I knew I didn't have long with him.

> Whenever a woman is in labor, she has pain, because her hour has come; but when she is delivered of the child, she no longer remembers the anguish, for joy that a child is born into the world. (John 16:21)

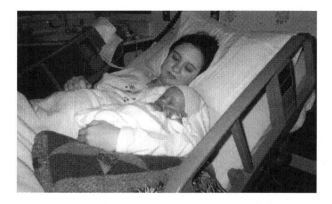

CHAPTER

6

I MADE THE CALL LATER THAT DAY TO TAMMY AND RICKIE TO tell them that he had arrived. I could hear the excitement in their voices as I told them all about him. They would not be meeting him for a few more days, so I wanted to share the news with them. I glossed over how tough the day had been and told them all the good things. I told them about his beautiful, blue eyes and porcelain skin. I told them he had ten perfect fingers and ten perfect toes. I told them he was the most beautiful baby I had ever seen. I knew they had been hoping and praying for this day for a long time and I wanted to share everything about him with them. I didn't tell them I was trying to etch these things in my memory as I looked at him. I didn't tell them that holding him was the most love I had every felt in my heart and that I wasn't sure I'd be able to let him go. I didn't tell them all my worries and fears. I kept it light and happy in my voice for them, a skill I'd get better at as time went on: hiding my true feelings.

There were lots of visitors in and out over the next few days in the hospital. Friends and family who were in town for the holidays would stop by. I had almost forgotten it was Christmas time. I honestly don't remember giving or receiving any gifts that year. I had a few other things on my mind. What I do remember is the outpouring of love and concern from my friends and most of my family. I mentioned that I came from a large family previously, and many of them were in town for Christmas. There were still those few who were not supportive and pretty much pretended that I didn't exist, but the supportive ones far exceeded the non supportive ones at the time. I was so emotional during that time and felt on the verge of a breakdown at any moment, but each visit with my support system gave me hope. Hope that I would be able to do this and that things would work out in the end. Their love and support meant so much to me. Each visit in the hospital was a gift, and I know God was loving me through all of them.

I spent as much time with the baby over those two days in the hospital as I could. The nurses were still apprehensive to bring him, but I insisted. The hospital social worker even came in to discuss it. No matter how hard it was, I will always treasure those few days where he was only mine and I could see and hold him as much as I wanted. I knew letting go of him would be difficult, but it was going to be hard no matter when I did it, so I held onto him while I could.

The time finally came on Christmas Eve to go home from the hospital. I woke up that morning with a sick feeling in my stomach. I didn't want to go. I didn't want my time to come to an end. I knew he was going to a foster family close by for a few days until the adoption could be finalized and I could visit him, but I also knew it wouldn't be the same. Here he was all mine. I had many moments of questioning myself. Could I really do this? Was I strong enough? The answer to those questions was and still is no. I can't do it on my own, and I am not strong enough. With God though, I was able to walk out of the hospital.

That walk to the car and ride home was the toughest thing I had ever had to do up until this point in my life. Was this the right thing? Could I really leave him? I didn't want to. In that moment, I wanted to go get him from the nursery and bring him home with me. It took all the strength I had not to change my mind. I knew that God had called me to place him for adoption and that he had called Tammy and Rickie to be his parents, but that didn't make my heart feel better. This sweet baby was a part of me, and I wasn't sure I could let him go. I reluctantly got in the car without a baby in a car seat. Through tears, I watched the hospital disappear in the distance, with my sweet baby boy still in it. This was not how motherhood was supposed to be. I was screaming on the inside, "Take me back! I can't leave him!" but on the outside only sadness and tears showed. My mom drove me home with an empty back seat and an empty heart.

I spent a lot of time in my room over the next few days. Just because the baby didn't come home with me didn't mean I didn't experience all the afterbirth stuff. I had cramping, bleeding, and breast soreness from my milk coming in. I didn't know what to do with these things so I stayed in bed most of the time. The one time I came out of my room to be with family for Christmas, I went into the room where everyone was gathered. My parents, brother, aunts and uncles, grandmother, and all my cousins were laughing and hanging out like any other holiday. I just couldn't bring myself to get into the holiday spirit. One of my cousins was an infant and I could barely stand to look at her. It made me so sad and made me miss my baby so much. So I started what would be a long season of withdrawal and went back to my room to cry by myself.

Over the next few days, while he was at the foster family's home, my mom and I went to visit him often. At least once a day we would drive to their home and stay a while. This is probably the part of the story I would change if I could. You see, I had to wait five days after the birth to officially sign the adoption papers. I had three options for the baby during that time. I could have taken him home with me, let Tammy and Rickie have him early, or have a foster family keep him for those in between days. Selfishly, I chose the third option. I knew having him at my house would have been too hard, but I wasn't quite ready to let him go. He stayed with a wonderful family for those days, and they were kind enough to let me visit as often as I wanted. I was able to bathe him, feed him, and just be with him. It was good for my heart to do the "normal" motherhood things. I would hold him and rock him and just soak in all the moments I could. Every time we left, I couldn't wait to go back. This family was so wonderful to him and to me. They didn't have to let me into their home, but they could see I needed it and let me come and stay as long as I wanted.

I don't know if involving another family who would love and miss him was the right thing, but it was right for me at the time. It seems like maybe a selfish decision on my part, to deny Tammy and Rickie those first precious days, but it did my heart so much good. I needed that time to see him and hold him. I knew things would be different soon and I just needed more time. Time to just be his mom, time to bond, time to allow my heart to be ready for the next step, and time to come to terms with letting him go.

CHAPTER

THE DAY FOR LETTING MY SWEET BABY GO CAME FASTER THAN I thought. I blinked and my time with him was coming to an end. It was what I call Placement Day, December 28, 1998. With the help of the people at the VOA, I had planned a ceremony in which I would hand over the baby. Suggestions had been given to me to just say my goodbyes and let them give the baby to Tammy and Rickie. I did not like these suggestions. I wanted to be a part of this moment for him and for them. I wanted to be strong enough to hand him over myself. I wanted to see the joy in their faces. I had invited a priest to come and pray over all of us. My parents, grandmothers, best friend, and the priest were all going to be there for support. Everything was ready.

The foster family had brought the baby in a little early so that his father could see him one more time and he could say his goodbyes. He had gone to see him at some point in the hospital, but our paths did not cross. We were not speaking at this point, so he was not going to be present at the ceremony. He had finally agreed to sign the papers and consent to the adoption, and I was grateful for that. I know that it must have been a difficult day for him too, but at the time, his feelings were the last thing I was worried about. By the time I arrived, he had already signed the papers and gone. I was glad to have one less stress that day. I see how selfish that was of me now. Maybe I should have included him in the events of the day. It's easy to look back and see the mistakes I made, but in the moment, I didn't give it a second thought.

I had packed up all the gifts I had been given throughout the pregnancy for the baby to give to Tammy and Rickie. It wasn't much, a few outfits and blankets, but I wanted them to have them. I wanted to feel like I was contributing to his life and upbringing after today. I wanted any piece of me to remain with him. I also had written him a letter at the suggestion of the counselor. It was something he would read when he discovered he was adopted and who I was. I had rewritten this letter many times over the last few weeks. I probably could've written a book with all the thoughts and emotions I had. I wanted him to know the reasons for this decision of adoption and to know how much I loved him from the moment of conception. I hope those feelings came across when he finally read it.

I had a little time with the baby before Tammy and Rickie were to arrive. It may have been five minutes, or it may have been an hour, but I wanted time to stand still. I held him, rocked him, and stared at him the whole time. I wanted to memorize his features and remember the feel of him in my arms. I knew I would see him again, but I also knew that when I did, he would be theirs and I'd only be a visitor. Never again would he be only my son.

When they told me that Tammy and Rickie arrived, my heart began to race. I held him a little tighter and stood up to get ready for them to walk in. When they walked in, the whole feeling in the room changed. A peace came over me that I wish I could get back to. It was as if I felt God's plan being fulfilled. As sad as I was and as hard as it was going to be, I knew it was exactly where I was supposed to be. They were so excited to see him and finally hold him. I hugged him one last time and kissed his forehead. I whispered to him, "I love you and always will. Now meet your new mom and dad." With those words, I handed him over to them. As I let go and felt my heart break, I could see the pure joy filling theirs. With tears in all our eyes and on our cheeks, the three of us stood there and hugged. I see now that God had brought them to me for him and that he would be so loved.

The priest that was there gathered us around and prayed over all of us. It brought me so much comfort to have him there to bless my son and his new family. You know when people say, "People may not remember the words you say, but they will remember how you make them feel." This is so true. I don't remember any of the words anyone said that day. I do remember Tammy and Rickie making me feel like I belonged and was loved by them. We were basically strangers; those feelings don't make sense. How could these people love me so much already and love my son at first sight? I mean the second part was a no-brainer. He was the most beautiful baby ever born. I had been so worried they would get him and run out and never speak to me again. I could see already that this would not be the case. They had decided to name him Reed Jarred—Jarred after St. Gerard, who is the patron saint of expectant mothers. That was the medal she had given me when we first met. I loved his name and thought it was perfect. I found out later that Reed is a family name on my mom's side of the family, so it was even more perfect of a fit.

We didn't stay very long after I handed him over. I knew they needed time with him and had to travel back home. I hugged the foster family, who had stayed for the ceremony, and thanked them for taking such good care of him. I thanked the priest and all the workers at the VOA who helped. Then I said goodbye to Tammy and Rickie, and their new son.

My peace quickly faded as my aching heart wanted to stay in this moment and this place forever. I didn't know what would happen next. I had so many worries and fears about the future. Would he know me? Would they really let me see him? Would they love him with everything they had? Was this the right thing? I had to trust God's plan for all of us. I had to trust that God would heal my broken heart and wounded spirit. I walked out of there scared, unsure, broken, and feeling alone. I felt no hope for me. I needed to trust God, but I could not feel his presence. I didn't see that he had a bigger plan. All I saw was hopelessness and the thought of *What now?*

> I waited patiently for the Lord; he inclined to me and heard my cry. (Psalm 40:1)

CHAPTER

8

THE FIRST FEW DAYS AFTER PLACEMENT DAY PASSED VERY slowly. I spent most of my time in my room alone, not wanting to interact with anyone. It was easier to be alone than to pretend I was OK or explain my sadness over and over. When friends would call, I would lie and say I was fine and just wanted to be at home. I was far from fine. I didn't cry much in that time; I was just numb and wanted to be alone.

I was sitting at home alone on New Year's Eve, watching some random TV show in my room, when my friends came to drag me out of the house to go to a party. I resisted and told them no one wanted to hang out with me, but they insisted. They told me they refused to leave me there alone. Reluctantly, I got dressed and out we went. The party was at a friend's camp. Most of the people there were several years older than us and I hoped they didn't know about the baby and adoption, though being from a small town, I'm sure they knew. There were music, a bonfire, food, and lots of fold-up chairs all over the place. Nothing fancy, just friends hanging out. It was easy to slump into a chair and blend in. I wasn't forced to make conversation. I just observed everyone going on with normal life. I wondered what normal life would be for me now. I have to admit it was nice to have a change of scenery.

It was getting to be late in the night and there were just a few of us left by the campfire. One of the older guys I didn't really know asked me where my baby tonight was. I was speechless for a minute, and then I just spilled my guts and told him about the adoption. I cringed on the inside when I was finished, thinking, *What have I done?* I didn't know this guy, and here I was telling him details about my life. I think I just needed to say it out loud, like then it would be real. To my surprise, he didn't seem shocked. He said, "Oh, I didn't know all that. I'm sorry." It wasn't the reaction I expected. I expected people to be shocked and condemn me, but that wasn't the case at all. I was grateful for his kindness and glad I got out of the house that night.

My next few weeks of winter break passed without any major event. I mostly stayed home, with the occasional forced outing with my friends. Thank goodness for them. They would always show up just when I needed to be dragged out of my hole of self-pity. I was not looking forward to the break ending and them going back to college while I was stuck at home.

By the time spring semester started, I was ready to get out of town. I arranged my class schedule to be off every Friday. I began living two lives. My Monday through Thursday life was spent going to class and working on schoolwork. I had not really made friends at school because I had kept to myself so much when I was pregnant, so I didn't really have anything to stick around for. Friday through Sunday, I was in Baton Rouge with my friends at LSU. I would stay with them, and we would go out and party. I had kind of a don't-care attitude. My grades seemed unimportant, which meant I didn't work as hard. All I wanted to do was get out of town and be with my friends. I didn't do anything reckless. I just wanted to be where not everyone knew my story and asked how I was doing all the time. While I was thankful my parents had become so supportive, sometimes I felt like they were smothering me a little with all the questions about how I was doing. I just wanted to be a normal college kid for a while, and that meant getting out of town.

There was another ulterior motive for my wanting to be in Baton Rouge. Tammy and Rickie lived nearby, and I hoped they would let me visit them. We had talked on the phone a few times, but I was anxious to see them again. I just knew it would do my heart some good. My moods had been up and down since placement day, and I was hoping to regain some of the peace I had felt that day. They agreed to meet with me on one of my first visits to Baton Rouge at a local restaurant.

I was so nervous for this visit. I asked two of my friends to go with me to see him as support. While I was excited to see him, I had so many worries too. I wondered if he had changed much since I saw him last. I wondered if he would recognize my voice. I wondered if he would feel the same in my arms. We arrived early to get a table and wait for them to arrive. I was a ball of nerves. As usual, all these fears washed away when they walked in and that same peace flooded me. He was just as perfect as I remembered, and maybe it was just me, but he seemed to recognize my voice.

While my friends and I took turns holding him, we talked with Tammy and Rickie about life and school. They were so easy to talk to and seemed truly interested in my life now. The conversation flowed as if we had known each other forever. Holding him in my arms was the greatest gift of the visit though. I had missed him and felt so blessed to be able to see and hold him again. I am so grateful still for the kindness they showed me in letting me see Reed so much. It would have been easy for them to say no and cut me out of his life, but God had a different path for us. I cherished every second they let me spend with him, and it always passed too quickly. I could've stayed in that moment forever, but unfortunately, they had to leave soon. After hugging all of them one more time, we parted ways.

Tammy and Rickie sensed how much I needed these visits and would agree to them every few weeks. I eventually began to go by myself, not needing the support as much. They made me feel like I was a member of their family. Each time we parted was hard. It was like leaving the hospital all over again. My heart would break every time. That part never got easier, but the reassurance I got at each visit that he was in good hands would sustain me until the next visit. I wondered about him every single day, and still do, but knowing he was loved eased my pain, if only a little.

During my double-life college semester, my friends and I decided to go to New Orleans for Mardi Gras. There was a party around every block. The first parade we went to was a night parade. We set out to meet up with friends, watch the parade, and catch the coveted beads. For the first time in months, I did not dwell on my grief; I was merely in the moment. The sights of people dressed in costume and gathering with their friends, along with the sounds of laughter and talking with old friends, kept me well distracted.

At this particular party was that guy, the one who had asked about my baby on New Year's Eve. We talked for a minute as we walked to the parade route. He was so easy to talk to. Neither of us had any agenda, just two people at the same place at the same time. These parades and parties last for hours, so there were several times we ended up standing in the same spot. At one point, I was even sitting on his shoulders trying to vie for the better beads. When the parade ended, we each went with our own groups without a second thought of the other. I wasn't in a place to even think about boys or relationships, so it was easy to keep things light. But I did like the fact that there was no judgment in his voice when he talked to me, even though he knew my story. God was working on my heart even when I didn't have it open to him.

A few weeks later, I was in my usual weekend town of Baton Rouge with my friends. We headed to a party at a friend's house, and who was there but the same guy. I knew that we both lived in Alexandria, and it was funny that we kept running into each other out of town. He was talking with one of my friends and mentioned that he wanted to take dance lessons in Alexandria but didn't have anyone to take with him. I heard my friend say, "Tracy lives there; you should ask her." When he didn't say anything about it to me at the party, I assumed he didn't want to ask me and there was no way he'd call me. Who would want to hang out with me anyway? I wasn't exactly wonderful company most of the time.

Despite my negative thoughts, he did call me a few days later and asked if I wanted to go to dance lessons with him. I could not believe that he actually called. I decided to take a leap and say yes, even though it was way out of my comfort zone. I was so nervous when he picked me up for the first class. We had only had three conversations; I barely knew him. When I got in his truck, I was instantly at ease. There was no pressure, no agenda, and no need for forced conversation. We talked like two friends just hanging out. I still wasn't ready for any type of relationship, so this was perfect.

We were the youngest people in the dance class by about twenty years and the only ones not married. It was a little awkward when we had to hold hands for the dances; we would immediately drop hands when the song ended. The classes were every week and we learned lots of dances like the waltz, cha-cha, two-step, and our favorite: the jitterbug. We were actually pretty good. I'm still not sure if we were really good or just good compared to the old people in our class. Either way, it was lots of fun and something I started looking forward to each week. We became more comfortable with one another and even started going to dinner after class some weeks.

This type of friendship was so foreign to me. All the other boys I had been out with wanted one thing only and made that very clear. We never had real conversations or went on real dates. Were these dates? Did he think so? Was I ready for dates? I wasn't sure so I kept it light and going just like it was. I was afraid if we made it a relationship, it would change and there would be expectations that I wasn't ready for.

After a few months of dance lessons, and even a few non dance night dinners, I decided I was ready. We had dinner plans, and I was going to ask him if we were dating. Did he want a relationship, and what did that mean to him? I was so nervous that I could barely eat. I was nervous not because I didn't think he wanted a relationship but because I didn't know what his expectations would be. I had decided the next time I was intimate with a man would be on my wedding night and I needed to tell him this up front. I didn't know if it would be a deal breaker for him. But I didn't get the nerve to ask him at dinner. I chickened out.

As I sat in his truck on the way home, beating myself up for being chicken, I finally got the nerve to ask. "What are we doing here?" I said. He said, "Um, what do you mean?" In my best thirteen-year-old feeling self, I said, "Do you like me? I like you." He said, "Yes, I like you." "So are we dating?" I asked. "I guess so," he said. So mature, right. Like every girl dreams. But it was enough for me for now. I knew that I could trust him and that he was different from any boy I had ever dated. I felt sure there would be no pressure from him to do anything I didn't want to do. I knew in that moment that God had sent me Jimmy, who was exactly what I needed when I needed it.

> We know that in everything God works for good with those who love him, who are called according to his purpose. (Romans 8:28)

CHAPTER

9

G OD HAD BEEN SENDING ME WHAT I CALL GOD-WINKS SINCE I had Reed. Sometimes I saw them; most times I didn't. My relationship with him, at least on my end, had been rocky. Growing up, my faith was very strong. I came from a large Catholic family. We went to church every week without fail. We prayed at night, and I felt like I had a strong faith base. The events of the past year had pretty much rocked my world, including my faith world. My strong Catholic family was not the support I expected, and I felt immense shame and guilt around them. The shame and guilt spread into all aspects of my life, especially when it came to God. My life seemed to be lived one moment to the next without much thought given to what I was doing. I certainly did not give any thought to what God might be doing in my life. Actually, I did not think about God often. When I did, I felt such shame that I would quickly redirect my thoughts. Going to Mass and praying were not priorities in my life at this time as they once had been. The guilt of how I had failed God was so strong any time I walked into church that I would barely go. I felt very alone, and I felt as if God had abandoned me in my time of need. When I was home on Sundays, I would go to church with my parents. The place I had grown up and felt comfortable in felt foreign to me. I felt the eyes looking at me and heard the whispers. I kept my head down and hurried to the car when it was over. Most weekends I would make sure I stayed out of town on Sundays so that I didn't have to go.

I could not see past my own feelings to see the good God was doing in my life. Instead of seeing the joy I had brought to another family through adoption, I saw that I was careless and had made a mistake. Instead of seeing the life I had given birth to, I saw grief and sorrow. My vision was so clouded with my own thoughts and feelings that I saw no good in my actions. I definitely didn't feel deserving of any graces from God. The words "I'm so proud of your decision" stung. I thought, *Proud? Hardly.* While I was thankful that my parents were proud of my decision and supported me, I did not accept their support wholeheartedly. As time went on, I began to resent them for not entertaining any thought of my keeping Reed. I don't know that it would have made any difference in my decision, but their silence on the subject was loud. I didn't ever say anything to them about my resentment. I just pulled away from them a bit. I could hardly stand for them to ask me how a visit went; I didn't feel they had the right to know. I can see now they did the best they could, but I couldn't see past my own pain at the time.

The Mother's Day after Reed was born was one of the worst days yet. All my friends had come home to be with their moms, so there was no escaping to Baton Rouge for the weekend. The two-year-old tantrum started early that morning in my head. *I don't want to celebrate this day!* I screamed in my mind. I wanted to hide under the covers in my bed and not come out until the next day. I was angry at this day.

My dad would have none of that. I was told to get up and get dressed because we were going to church. I didn't want to be part of any Mother's Day celebration, not for me or my mom. I sulked the whole way there and slumped in the pew when we sat down. I pretty much zoned out for the first part of the Mass. The priest rambled on in the homily about the joys of motherhood and all its blessings. I certainly didn't want to hear all that. At the end of the homily, he had all the mothers stand to give them a blessing. I was not ready for the unexpected heartache that came with those words. I could not stand; I was not officially a mom. Yes, I had given birth, but someone else was getting to be called mom. My heart ached in that moment for what could've been. Silent tears rolled down my cheeks as he blessed the moms in the congregation. I wanted so badly to stand. I also wanted to run out of there quickly.

After that day, it was hard to go back. I just didn't feel like God could love someone like me, so I withdrew and only went to church when forced by my parents. I pulled away from the love of the Father, but he kept pulling me back in with his God-winks and blessings.

CHAPTER

10

My next blessing from God came in the form of the best visit yet with Reed. Over the past few months since he was born, I had visited with them at least once a month. Tammy and Rickie were so gracious in their allowing me to be a small part of their lives. Reed was growing and developing the most precious personality. Maybe it was just wishful thinking, but he always seemed to remember me. The weeks between visits seemed so long and the visits never long enough. The longing to be with him more and more grew stronger. I hoped those feelings would diminish as time went on, but they only seemed to deepen.

This particular visit was going to be different. My parents and Jimmy were moving me into an apartment in Baton Rouge. I had decided to transfer to LSU to be with my friends, and I just needed a change. Since everyone would be in town, we decided to meet up with Tammy, Rickie, and Reed. This was the first time my parents had seen him since placement day and the first time ever for Jimmy. I was so nervous that day. I wasn't sure what to expect. I knew in my heart that it would be great, but there was always that fear lurking beneath the surface waiting to show up.

We decided on a local restaurant to meet for lunch. My parents, Jimmy, and I got there early to get a table. It was a Sunday afternoon so the place was crowded with people. The smell of fresh hamburgers filled the air. I could see the excitement on my parents' faces as we waited. I hoped they couldn't see my nervousness. I was worried Jimmy would be overwhelmed and not be able to handle it. I was scared he wouldn't want to be with me anymore after witnessing all my emotions that would come after the visit. I knew I would be good during the visit but had gotten used to the emotional roller coaster that came on the drive home. I was usually by myself so no one had to see me. I knew he would see me cry that day and was scared he would run.

As usual, when Tammy, Rickie, and Reed arrived, a sense of peace flooded me. Reed immediately jumped into my arms and then quickly to my dad's. We laughed, talked, took pictures, and were content to just be. I constantly gave side-glances at Jimmy to check on how he was. He always had a smile on his face and seemed to be comfortable. He interacted and visited with Tammy and Rickie like they had known each other for years. Just witnessing his ease in the situation put so many of my worries to rest. As I looked at him that day, fully engaged, no judgment, and willing to be a part of that part of me, I realized that I loved him and that God had truly sent him to me.

After we had eaten, I knew the visit would be ending soon and I began to get the all too familiar pit in my stomach. I would have to leave him again. Oh, it was so hard every time. We hugged and said goodbye. I hugged my parents; they were heading back home and thanked them for coming today and being there. Then I walked with Jimmy to his truck. Once in the truck, the tears began to fall. He let me cry silently and reached for my hand. He didn't need to say a word; just his presence was enough. He didn't tell me to stop or try to make me feel better. He was just there for me. He was the calm presence I needed that day and for many days to come.

Finally, all of you, have unity of spirit, sympathy, love of the brethren, a tender heart, and a humble mind. (1 Peter 3:8)

CHAPTER 11

My first semester at LSU went by quickly. I enjoyed living away from home and the freedom that came with that. I settled into a routine of school, work (I worked at a local daycare), and parties on the weekends. Jimmy came to visit pretty often, and we continued dating. My job was not one that I loved. I am not a natural teacher, but I loved being around the kids. I think I chose that job to be close to kids and maybe be able to mother them, if only a little. I developed special bonds with a few of them and maybe it made me miss Reed a little less.

I saw Reed every few weeks or so. If it would've been up to me, I would have seen him every day, but I didn't want to overstep my boundaries. Being in the same town made him seem so close, yet so far. I talked to Tammy regularly. We would talk about Reed and how he was doing, but we would talk about life too. She was quickly becoming one of my closest confidants. I could tell her anything. Sometimes I would call her during the two-hour drive home for the weekend and we would talk to whole way. She never seemed annoyed by my calling and was always willing to talk and listen. She truly made me feel like part of the family.

As Reed's birthday approached, I became nervous. All the usual doubts began to creep in. Would they let me see him? Would he remember me? I also didn't have any idea what to expect emotionally.

I was worried I would have a meltdown on his birthday. Tammy and I talked and decided I could come visit them at their house on the morning of his birthday. I had not been to their home before now. I was very curious as to what it would be like. Would it be warm and inviting or cold and modern? I hoped it would be a cozy home with lots of love in the air. I wondered what his room looked like and what color it was. What his bed looked like and what chair they rocked him in. I wondered if they sat at a fancy dining table or just at a breakfast bar to eat. I wondered if they had a big backyard with lots of room to run and play. I couldn't wait to go there and see them all and find out for myself.

The morning of December 22, 1999, I traveled to Reed's home to see him for his first birthday. This morning drive was much different from the one I had taken a year ago. On my drive over, I reflected on the past year. So much had happened. I felt like I had grown ten years. While my life was far from perfect, and I still had many days filled with sadness, I was full of hope this day. Hope that the next year and years to come would bring more visits and us closer. Hope that my heart would continue to heal. Hope that Reed would feel the love we all had for him.

When I arrived, they came out to meet me. Their home was exactly like I had hoped. It was warm and cozy. It was not a large home but sat off the road on a large piece of property. There were trees everywhere and lots of places for a little boy to play outside. It was perfect. I imagined that Reed liked to be outside more than in. He ran to me and jumped into my arms. I gave him the biggest hug I could and wished him a happy birthday. I felt my heart grown when he hugged me back. This was exactly where I wanted to be.

We sat outside most of the time at a picnic table and talked while Reed ran around in the yard. It was a beautiful day with the sun shining. Even though it was a beautiful day, I still wanted to go inside their home. When we finally went inside, I saw that it was a small, cozy, and warm home. The kitchen and living room were one big room and it was not fancy or modern, which I liked. It felt like a home. I did not get to go in his bedroom, but I saw enough of their home to know Reed was comfortable and loved there.

I couldn't stay long because I was traveling back home for the holidays and they were getting ready for a birthday party. I hugged all three of them and said goodbye before getting in my car to head home. As I drove away, I saw the three of them standing together in the driveway. They looked like the perfect little family, like they belonged on the cover of a family magazine. I was so relieved that they were so happy and that Reed had so many people who loved him. His little family was better than I could have hoped for. He was healthy, happy, and loved. I could not help but be sad for what might have been though. I thought on my way home of how our lives would be different had I made a different choice. Would we have been as happy as they are? I couldn't let myself go down that road for too long; it was not the path God had for me. Although I grieved for what might have been, I was happy to know they were celebrating his life big and would be for years to come.

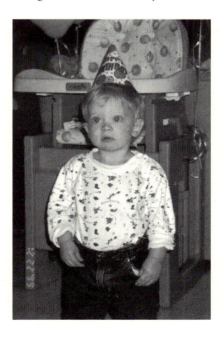

CHAPTER

12

After Christmas break, I returned to Baton Rouge and life went on as usual with school, work, and occasional visits with Reed. I was starting to get comfortable with our routine and felt secure in our relationship. I thought if it could just stay like this, I could make it. Then one day in the middle of the week, my phone rang. It was Tammy on the other end. There wasn't anything unusual about that, we called each other regularly, but there was something different in her voice. She asked if I wanted to meet up that week, and without hesitation, I said yes. I never passed on the opportunity to see them. The tone in her voice had been a little different. Maybe I should have read into it, but I brushed it off as nothing and headed to the mall.

For the past few months since I had been living in Baton Rouge, we had met up every few weeks. We always met at a neutral location, a restaurant, or something similar. Now that Reed was getting more active, our favorite spots were McDonald's playground or the mall. There was a carousel at the mall and plenty of room for a one-year-old to run around. We would often spend thirty minutes going up and down the escalators. I never tired of seeing his precious smile as he would look up at me and say, "Again." I couldn't resist him. That particular day we had decided on the mall.

My ride from my apartment that day seemed to take forever.

It was only a ten-minute drive to the mall and there was minimal traffic on the road. I kept playing the conversation with Tammy over and over in my mind. I couldn't shake the feeling that she was about to tell me something important. My immediate reaction was it must be bad news. Maybe they had had enough and didn't want to see me anymore. This was always my knee-jerk response to change; it must be bad. I don't know why. I guess things were going so well that I was waiting for the shoe to drop. I pushed that thought out and told myself I was reading too much into it, but I couldn't help but be a little nervous.

As I walked up to our usual meeting spot, I saw Tammy standing at the bottom of the escalators with an empty stroller. My heart skipped a beat for a second before I looked where her eyes were directed and saw a cute, blond-haired, blue-eyed boy peeking around the top of the escalators with the biggest smile on his face. I don't know whether it was getting to go down by himself or seeing me, but his face brightened as I walked up. I hugged Tammy as we waited for him to get to the bottom and then I scooped him up in my arms. We headed back up the escalator after he pleaded, "Again." After a few more trips, Tammy put him in the stroller and suggested we walk around.

The noises, smells, and people in the mall all slowly disappeared as we walked and talked. She was such an easy person to talk to, I always felt like I could tell her anything. I'm sure she was tired of hearing my tales of school and living with three other girls, but she never showed it. She always made a point ask how I was doing, *really doing,* which was comforting. She talked to me about her work and how Reed was doing. She never talked about any of the hard parts of motherhood, only the good. She always beamed when she talked about Reed and that made my heart happy.

After we had walked a while, she stopped and turned to me. She said, "I need to tell you something." She had a very serious look on her face, and I think my stomach fell out of my body doing flips. After what seemed like an eternity she said, "I'm pregnant."

I was excited and nervous at the same time. I hugged her immediately and told her how excited I was for her and Rickie. I had never wanted Reed to be an only child, so I truly was excited for them all. I could tell she was relieved to see my excitement. Her serious face immediately turned into a joyful grin.

We never talked too much about her fertility issues other than surface information in the beginning. She told me how she had never been regular her whole life and that they were unable to conceive because of that. She said that the month after they adopted Reed, she became regular and had been ever since. She said they weren't trying to get pregnant, that it had just happened. I could see the pure joy in her eyes and on her face. I was so happy that she was happy.

If I'm honest, I was scared too. I knew that they loved Reed, but what would this new baby change. My mind was going in a million different directions. What if this new baby changed how they felt about Reed? What if having a baby of their own made them love Reed less? What if a new baby meant less time for me to visit with them? I was scared to be pushed out of their lives. I had grown to need not only to see Reed but Tammy as well. So many questions, so many unknowns. Then I saw the way she looked at Reed asleep in the stroller and my mind eased. She loved him with all her heart and a new baby wouldn't change that. God would give them enough love to go around. I knew in my heart that all would be well.

CHAPTER

13

After one semester at LSU, I decided I didn't want to be premed anymore. Something just told me it wasn't right. Four years of undergrad, four years of med school, then residency seemed to be too long before starting a family. I thought after having Reed that I would be on the career path and that family would come much later. But as time passed, I felt God calling me to the vocation of motherhood. My relationship with Jimmy was progressing and I could certainly see myself marrying him one day. I made an appointment with an advisor and planned to ask about nursing.

I knew with nursing I could still help people and be in the medical field. I also knew that I could start the next chapter of my life sooner. I had not thought about the fact that I may not be able to stay in Baton Rouge to compete this. When I met with my advisor, she told me that I would have to transfer to another location to pursue a nursing degree. I did not want to leave Baton Rouge and the closeness to Reed. I had settled into a routine of good days leading up to a visit of joy, hope and happiness followed by days or weeks of loss and depression. What was I going to do without those good days? Would I fall deep in my hole of self-pity, shame, and depression? Change is scary, but God called me to move to Lafayette to pursue a degree in nursing.

In August 2000, I moved to attend ULL for nursing. This

would be my third college in three years. I often use the Goldilocks comparison when telling people about my college experience. The first one was too small, the second one too big, and the third one was just right. After just one semester there, I was admitted to the nursing school. I finally felt like my life and future was taking shape.

Jimmy and I continued to date. He was very supportive of me continuing to go to school. He would come visit me almost every weekend and we talked on the phone every day. I knew at this point that we would get married someday, but I wanted to finish school and get my degree first.

At both LSU and ULL, I found jobs at daycares. I could say it was for the hours and no weekends, but I just wanted to be around kids. I missed Reed and thought about him every day. Being around other kids made me miss him a little less. It was harder to see him while living in Lafayette than it had been in Baton Rouge.

Nursing school was way more intense than I had anticipated. I spent many hours studying and practicing for exams. Thank goodness in my time there I had developed a great group of friends to go through it with. We would often study together and then celebrate together with $1 margaritas at El Chico after exams. We even went to Mass a few times together. The campus church was right next to the nursing building. This was no mistake; we definitely needed the prayers. Sadly, I did not go as often as I should have and missed many Sunday Masses. I was still struggling with my faith and just wasn't ready to work on it yet. I still felt shame when I walked in church and felt I didn't belong there.

I know God was with me in those days because there was no way I could have handled all that on my own, but I didn't feel him then. I was so clouded with stress and sadness that I could not feel his love and mercy. I was so blinded by my own mess that I could not see his hand in everything. I know he carried me through many of my exams. I know he would have Jimmy call me at just the right moment that I was about to have a breakdown from stress. I know he would have Tammy call me when I was missing Reed the most to update me on his day-to-day life. He placed all those people in my path and I still didn't see it. I was so angry with myself for "falling" that I couldn't see who had caught me. I spent many of those nursing school days blocking out my grief that I became almost obsessed with doing well. I felt like I had to prove to people that my life would have meaning. I would show that I used my second chance well. I would be successful despite my past. I got so wrapped up in all that that I kind of lost me for a while. I'm not sure if I was trying to prove this to others or to myself. I think I felt I needed to make the rest of my life seem good to make up for my mistakes. I don't know why I couldn't just ask for forgiveness for my mistakes and accept myself for who I was. It might have made life simpler in those days, but I pressed on with the pursuit of success.

CHAPTER

14

AFTER THREE YEARS OF LONG-DISTANCE RELATIONSHIP, I KNEW I would marry Jimmy eventually. I knew my family had given him an heirloom diamond to use. What I didn't know was when he would propose. His mom had planned a surprise birthday party for him, or so I thought, in the middle of a school week. I headed home to be there. As I was stalling to get ready at his apartment, he called me into his room. When I walked in, he was on one knee with a box in his hand. I was totally surprised, and it is hard to surprise me, that he was proposing on his birthday. I quickly said yes! He said the surprise party was actually to celebrate our engagement. How sweet was that for him to share his birthday celebration with the news of our engagement. We walked into his mom's house and no one was surprised. They all knew, except for my mom. My dad had not told her. She can't keep a secret. It was a wonderful night celebrating us.

The next year was super busy. I was trying to finish up nursing school while planning a wedding, and for some reason, we decided to build a house too. I did not have a lot of time for anything else, including visits to Baton Rouge. I talked to Tammy quite often, and they were very happy for me and Jimmy, but talks were not the same as visits.

As the days of graduation and the wedding approached, my joy of all the good things happening in my life was mixed with a bit of sadness and longing. I had been working so hard to prove myself and here I was doing it. I was happy to be graduating and marrying Jimmy, but I felt like I was moving on without part of me. Oftentimes I felt like I didn't deserve to be happy and should feel lonely and miserable all the time. I just couldn't seem to move past all the wrongs I had done and allow myself to feel the happiness. What I should have done was ask God to help me heal and continue living. Instead I tried to do it on my own. I put on a happy face and pretended that life was perfect.

Graduation day was amazing. When I walked across the stage to receive my diploma, I thought about all the wonderful friends I had made there and all the support they had given me. I knew some of them would be lifelong friends even though we would all go our separate ways. Finishing nursing school was definitely a group effort. The feeling of accomplishing something I had worked so hard for was incredible. I felt like a real adult. My family came to celebrate with lunch after the ceremony. It was one of my last days in Lafayette and I was looking forward to moving back home to be closer to all of them. While I was sad to leave my friends, I was ready to get started with the next chapter of my life.

After graduation came the craziness of the holidays followed immediately by the wedding. There were not that many things left to do, but I felt very stressed trying to get it all done. The holidays were tough every year anyway with Reed's birthday right in the middle, so this year was on another level. I had built up in my mind the hope that Tammy and Rickie would bring Reed to the wedding. I hoped he could be a small part of my day. I didn't want to put any pressure on them to do anything they weren't comfortable with, so I didn't ask.

Our wedding was one of the most beautiful occasions I had ever been to. Surrounded by our family and friends, we committed to do life together. I felt so blessed to have found someone like Jimmy who supported me no matter what and accepted all of me. He had held my hand and wiped my tears many times and still wanted to marry me. How did I get so lucky?

While the wedding was wonderful and we had so much fun, I felt like it wasn't complete. Reed was always in the back of my mind. I still wasn't sure how to navigate this situation. Do I talk about him? Not talk about him? Was I supposed to forget him and move on? I just felt stuck there. He was a part of me, and his birth made me who I am. I did not and could not forget about him.

> What therefore God has joined together, let not man put asunder. (Mark 10:9)

CHAPTER 15

Since giving birth to Reed, my biological clock had been ticking and my dream of a family of my own was something I wanted so badly. Six months after we got married, Jimmy and decided to start trying to get pregnant. We weren't really in a hurry and just trusted it would happen when the time was right. A few months after trying, I was back in the bathroom staring at the stick and waiting for it to tell me my future. This time, I waited with hopeful anticipation instead of fear. Oh, what a difference a few years had made. The last time I watched the stick, I hope and prayed for it to be one line; this time, I prayed for two. When the second line popped up, I squealed with delight and ran to show Jimmy. We hugged and hurriedly called our parents to share the good news. What joy there was in sharing the news this time. There was no shame or guilt, only happiness.

Over the next few days, we continued to share our news with our family and friends. We were over the moon excited and wanted everyone to know. My first doctor's appointment went well; all my labs looked good. We didn't do an ultrasound because I was so early. I was about six weeks along and due in summer of 2005.

Everything was going well. I wasn't even sick, which should have been my first clue. One day while I was at work as a nurse in a labor and delivery unit, I began to have stomach pains. The pains continued to get worse as the day progressed. I began to worry that something may be wrong. My fears were confirmed when I went to the bathroom and saw the bleeding. Tears welled up and began to roll down my cheeks as I realized what was happening. I was losing this baby. My coworkers called my doctor, and he ordered an ultrasound. By the time the ultrasound was done, Jimmy had arrived to be with me. We both cried when they told us I was in fact having a miscarriage.

How could this be happening to me? I was ready this time. I had everything planned out. Wasn't it my turn to have a family? Was God punishing me for giving my first baby away? This last question haunted me and was all I could think about. The shame and sadness all came flooding back and doubled the grief I felt. I had a perfect, healthy baby and had given him away, and now it felt as if God was not going to give me another chance. I did not turn to God for help or healing in my sadness. Instead I became very bitter. The joy I had found in my job of helping to bring life into the world was now a daily reminder of what I didn't have. All my friends were having babies. My sister-in-law was about to have her second baby in one year. I should have been happy for them, but I could barely stand to be around them. Everything reminded me of my loss. The holidays were especially hard that year. I did not visit Reed that year on his birthday or at Christmas. I just couldn't do it. I spent all my free time sulking in self-pity.

The doctor had told us to try to get pregnant again soon, but I wasn't so sure. When the pregnancy test came up positive two months later, I was cautiously happy. We decided to keep quiet this time and only tell our parents. I was still grieving from the miscarriage and just didn't believe that anything good could happen. Slowly, after a few weeks, I finally let myself be excited again. I started wondering what life would be like with a baby. We still were very cautious and only a few people even knew we were pregnant.

Then one day, just like before, I started having cramps at work. When I went to the bathroom and saw the bleeding, I felt numb.

I knew what it meant. This time I didn't need an ultrasound to confirm it. My heart knew this baby was already gone. My heart was broken, and I was angry. I was so angry with God. I wondered how he could let this happen to me twice. Hadn't I suffered enough? Why couldn't he let me have this joy?

We thought not telling a lot of people would be easier, but it was not. Now we were going through our grief alone. It is very difficult to tell someone you've had a miscarriage when they didn't even know you were pregnant. With little support, I sank deep into my own despair. My grief and thoughts were much darker this time. I was very resentful of my family and friends who had babies and mostly kept to myself. I wondered if I had married a man with whom I would not be able to have a child. What if I had given away my one chance? Could I live with myself if that was the case? I blamed myself for this loss and could not let it go. I was sad all the time. Going to work was painful. The daily reminder of the blessings others had was almost too much to bear.

Once again, I did not turn to Jesus in my suffering. I did not ask him for help. I wondered where his mercy was. I sure didn't feel it. I felt abandoned by him and punished. I thought maybe my past sins were too great for him to give me his mercy. I didn't ask for his mercy either though. I simply shut him out completely, like I was shutting everyone else out. I was shutting Jimmy out too. I'm sure he was hurting over the losses too, but I didn't care at the time. I was selfishly focused only on me and my grief. If only I had shared my feelings with Jimmy, maybe he could have lightened my load and we could have grieved together. Unfortunately, I kept it all bottled up inside, which only made me more bitter.

When I went to the doctor for a follow-up, he suggested that I had a hormone deficiency that is key to maintaining a pregnancy. He said obviously I didn't have trouble getting pregnant, just staying that way. I doubtfully agreed with him. I did not tell him how I felt God was punishing me or that maybe I wasn't supposed to be a mother. I just let him tell me his scientific reason. We decided we would try again with the addition of a hormone replacement to maintain a pregnancy. I was not hopeful this time and actually considered not trying for a while, but something told me to stay the course. God's little nudges were not so apparent to me then, but I'm sure that was the something that spoke to me. I reluctantly agreed.

At some point during the weeks following the second miscarriage, Jimmy suggested we go to Mass. We had been hit-or-miss Catholics since we'd gotten married. My shame had kept me from attending regularly for years and that had only increased since the miscarriages. While at Mass, I prayed for God to show us what to do. I asked him if motherhood was something he wanted for me. I told him how angry I was at him for not giving me what I wanted. I know that sounds petty, but it's how I felt at the time. Jimmy and I never really talked about it, but we began to go to Mass more regularly, not necessarily every week but more than we were going. We sat in the back as to not be noticed though. I could feel our faith growing ever so slowly. I felt more hopeful for the future as we leaned more on him.

In May 2005 came my third positive pregnancy test in less than a year. I was nervous. I will admit that this time my body felt different, more pregnant if that's something, but my mind and heart were very cautious. This time we told all our friends and family and asked them to pray for us and our family. We wanted as many people praying for a positive outcome as we could. Our first doctor's appointments went well, and we had an ultrasound that showed a little bean with a heartbeat around six weeks. Things were starting to look up.

CHAPTER

16

THE FIRST FEW MONTHS OF THIS PREGNANCY, I WAS SICK. NAUSEA came at all hours of the day. Whoever named it "morning sickness" had obviously never been pregnant because it came morning, noon, and night. When I told my doctor about how sick I had been, he responded, "Good." Good? What? I wanted to throat-punch him right there. Good? Ha! He said that the more nausea I had meant the more pregnancy hormones, which was a good sign of a healthy pregnancy. I thought, *OK, I can accept that, as long as it goes away eventually.* The sickness did make it feel real, and I wanted so badly for this one to be real. I wanted the happy ending I had been missing with my previous pregnancies.

Jimmy and I had planned a trip to Orlando with some friends before I got pregnant. We were going to Disney World and to visit his sister. We decided to still go, even though I wasn't sure how sick I would be and how much fun I would be to be around. Jimmy's sister had two children under two and our friends had an eight-month-old. Most of the days we were there I was so nauseated that I didn't want to get out of bed, but I tried to put on a happy face and participate.

Disney World is not the place for a sick pregnant person in the summer for sure. When we finally got to the day that we were going to stay at Jimmy's sister's house to rest, I was so relieved. The boys were all going to a race in another city so I was looking forward to just hanging out with the girls and the kids—in the air conditioning. I was not prepared for the conversations we would have that night.

Jimmy's sister had two children in one year, literally January and December, who were now eighteen months and six months old. Our friend had an eight-month-old but had unexpectedly lost her father recently. Needless to say, these two mothers were a little stressed out. After they had put the kids to bed, we sat around talking. They proceeded to tell me how awful motherhood was and that I shouldn't do it. They listed all the hard things that come along with being a parent. I just sat there and listened. I didn't know how to respond or what to say. "Too late. Already pregnant," I think is what I said. What I wanted to say was what a gift they had been given to be able to parent their children. That I couldn't wait to bring a baby home, to my house, from the hospital. I knew it wasn't going to be easy, but I was willing to take the bad with the good.

I must have replayed that conversation in my head a thousand times over the months leading up to giving birth. I realize now that these two ladies were placed in my life then to show me that life isn't a fairy tale, and it is hard. I have watched them both become some of the best, strongest mothers I know. I still look up to them and value our friendship.

Once the first trimester ended, I began to actually enjoy my pregnancy. This one was much different from being pregnant at eighteen. I didn't have to hide or feel ashamed. Our families were very excited. We invited our moms to join us for the ultrasound where we would find out if it was a girl or a boy. They brought me into the same room I had gone in seven years earlier. I was taken aback by the memories of that day. The room looked the same, but the feeling in the air was so different. Instead of fear and shame, I felt happy anticipation. When she told us it was a boy, I cried happy tears. I felt like God was truly giving me a second chance. I was having another baby boy, and this time I could bring him home. Seven years earlier when the ultrasound tech showed us Reed on the screen, I thought, *Oh no, it's really happening.* This time when she showed us the baby boy, my heart exclaimed, *Oh yay, this is really happening.* It's amazing how the same moment years apart can bring about such different emotions. I knew this baby was a gift from God and I was not going to waste it.

The months leading up to the birth, I did things I didn't get to do the first time. I registered for baby items, had showers, and prepared a nursery. It felt strange to me because these were things I had not done the last time. All these things brought me joy and sadness at the same time. I was so grateful for all the people who cared about me and this new baby. They showered us with so much love and gifts. This was very different from when I had been pregnant before. There were no showers or celebrations of his life. I hadn't picked out room colors, clothes, or bedding for him; someone else had gotten to do that.

Experiencing all this for the first time was so wonderful, but it showed me what I had missed before. I let my mind wander to what it would have been like to have a happy pregnancy the first time. Would it have changed the outcome? I still knew that Reed was where he was supposed to be, but having another baby made me question a bit. I compared everything to the first time I was pregnant, including how I felt, how I looked, how people treated me, and even what delivery would be like this time. I wondered if giving birth would be different. Would it be just as painful? I wasn't sure I was ready for all that again.

Near the end of my pregnancy, I became so nervous about the delivery. My delivery of Reed was very difficult physically and emotionally. I worried the delivery of this baby would be just as hard. I knew the circumstances this time were much different, but I only had difficulty to compare it to, which made me apprehensive.

In one of the last few weeks of my pregnancy, I had been having contractions on and off for a few days, but nothing was consistent. One day while I was getting ready to go to work, my contractions felt different. They were only a few an hour, but they were strong enough to make me stop and breathe through them. I was working nights in labor and delivery and decided to go to work anyway. There couldn't be a much safer place to be anyway, right? All night long while I worked, my contractions became closer and closer until I was contracting more often than the patient I was caring for.

When I got off work at 7 a.m., my contractions were three to five minutes apart so I checked in. I just knew today would be the day. My doctor happened to be out of town so another doctor covered for him. He agreed that today would be the day and went ahead and broke my water. I was prepared for the flood this time. It got real fast. Within a couple of hours, I was getting my epidural and was soon ready for delivery. The first delivery was such a long day physically and mentally and I figured this one would be the same. Boy, was I wrong. Before I knew it and could wrap my head around it, they were calling for the doctor for delivery. I wanted to say, "Wait. I'm not sure I'm ready," but I don't think that would have mattered. Ready or not, he was coming.

When the doctor arrived, he started talking to us and taking his time getting ready. When the nurse said, "Umm, Doctor," in a strange voice, I knew something was up. Suddenly, he jumped up and caught the baby barehanded. There was no time for gloves. This child wanted out. As soon as I saw him, I felt this wave of relief. Relief that he was healthy. Relief that he was finally here. Relief that I was going to take this one home with me. I began to cry—I mean ugly, sobbing cry. So much that the doctor asked me if I was OK and if these were happy tears. I reassured him that I was OK but could not stop the waterworks. I could barely see the baby for all the tears, but I held him so tightly. I could not believe that after everything, God was blessing me with such a miracle. Nothing else mattered at that moment in time. I held that perfect baby boy in my arms and did not want to let him go. I was so grateful that God was giving me another chance to be a mother.

Cody James was born on February 3, 2006, and was perfect.

We only spent one night in the hospital, and it was a whirlwind. Visitors were in and out. Cody was in and out. This time around, there was no whispering from the nurses when I wanted to hold him. I had a hard time letting others hold him. This baby was mine, and I was taking him home with me. I still couldn't believe it. My mind kept going back to the last time I was in the hospital. It was such a different time, but I kept wondering what it would have been like if I had kept Reed. Would there have been this much excitement from my family and friends? Once again, the hauntings of my past choices robbed me of some of the joy of that day's events.

When we packed up to head home from the hospital, I was a ball of nerves. I just couldn't shake it. Why on earth was I so nervous? Then it hit me. The last time I left the hospital after having a baby was one of the most difficult days of my life. I guess my subconscious was worried the same thing was about to happen. But it wasn't. I was getting to bring him home this time.

Jimmy bundled him up in his car seat, put him in my lap, and wheeled me out in the wheelchair to the car. After Jimmy fastened the seat in the car, I climbed in next to Cody. Jimmy said, "What are you doing?" I said, "I am not leaving his side. I want to ride home right beside him." As we drove away, the stress of the day and nervousness exploded in waterworks. I couldn't help it. I was just so relieved to be bringing him home. I stared at his perfect little face the whole way. This was how a ride home from the hospital was supposed to feel: happy and content.

> Every good endowment and every perfect gift is from above, coming down from the Father of lights with whom there is no variation or shadow due to change. (James 1:17)

CHAPTER 17

I will admit that when we got home with Cody, I felt so lost. How in the world was I supposed to keep this tiny baby safe and healthy? He didn't sleep well, which meant I didn't sleep well. There were many nights when both of us cried. I thought often of the conversation at my sister-in-law's house about the difficult parts of being a mom. They were so right, and so wrong. They were right that it was hard. I was sleep-deprived, and there were lots of expectations. But they were so wrong because it was worth every single bit. Even in the moments of wanting to give up, I could look at my sweet boy and know he was a blessing from God.

The first year of Cody's life was fast and slow, if that makes sense. We fell into a family routine of work, a little sleep, and quality time. Just when we were getting in a groove, I threw a wrinkle in the plan by deciding to go back to school to become a nurse practitioner. I had always wanted to do more with my career, and having Cody made me realize I wanted more children so I'd better finish school now. When Cody was just four months old, I added more to our schedule by starting online classes. I knew that he wouldn't remember this time in his life and wouldn't notice that I wasn't present for a lot of things. I noticed though. If I wasn't at work or sleeping, I was studying. I didn't leave much time for my family.

Jimmy was the best support I could've asked for. He was a great dad and enjoyed spending time with our son, who was growing so fast. He seemed to be doing everything early. Crawled at five months, walked at nine, and never stopped talking. With every new "thing" Cody did came a small sense of sadness though. As Cody would take his first step, I would wonder what Reed's first step was like. Was he smiling, fearful, laughing? Cody was such a joy to be around as a child that the sadness would be fleeting, but it was always there, lurking.

As Christmastime came around, I thought this year would be easier emotionally because now I had a family and maybe wouldn't miss Reed so much. That's what I get for thinking. It actually had the opposite effect on me and made it worse. I spent Reed's birthday that year in bed crying most of the day. Getting to experience all the firsts with Cody made me realize just how much I had missed out on with Reed. It was as if I thought magically things would be perfect once I had my own family, as if I wouldn't still have the pain of my past to deal with. Tammy and I still talked all the time, and I called her on his birthday like usual. I'm not sure how well I hid my sadness in my voice that year. She told me thank-you like she always did and told me she would give Reed a big hug and a kiss for me for his birthday.

Having a young child, working full time, and going to school full time didn't leave much room for anything else for a few years. We did not have a chance to visit Reed very often during that time. I talked to Tammy often though. She always asked how I was doing. Even in her busy life, she made time to check on me and make sure I was good. Our faith life was sort of stagnant. We went to church occasionally and didn't pray regularly. It felt like I was going through the motions of life just waiting for the next thing to happen.

I finished graduate school and got a job working in a family practice clinic. Jimmy and I decided now would be a good time to try to have another child. I was nervous. Life was already busy with a two-year-old and a new job. I was also traveling to my job one hour each way. I was nervous I couldn't spread myself any thinner.

I was scared that I wouldn't be successful at getting pregnant this time. Mostly I was scared that I was still trying to replace Reed, and nothing would come close to that. I also went back to the worry I had for Tammy when she told me she was pregnant and worried if I would have enough love to go around.

On the morning of Cody's third birthday, we discovered we were pregnant. We told everyone that day at his party and asked them to begin praying for a healthy pregnancy. I can see now that even though we weren't fully engaged in our faith, we knew it was important. Around that same time, we decided to make a resolution to attend Mass weekly. We sat in the back mostly, and quickly left afterward, but we were there. God was working on us, just slowly.

This pregnancy was much different from the other two. For the first four months, I was sick all the time. I had three hospitalizations for dehydration. Trying to work and take care of my family while being so sick proved to be very difficult. Sometime in the fifth month, I finally was able to eat and have a little more energy. I was very excited for this new baby and didn't really care if it was a boy or a girl. It seemed like having a girl would complete my family and that was what I had been trying to do since having Reed: have my own real family. I wanted my life to feel whole and was doing everything in my power to accomplish that. What I needed to do was just put my faith and trust in God and I would feel complete. Instead, I tried to take control, and nothing ever felt complete.

On the day of the ultrasound, Jimmy and I decided to bring Cody with us. We thought it would be a wonderful moment to share with him. He had been hopeful for a sister, until that day. That day, he decided he wanted a brother. Jimmy did not hide the fact that he wanted a boy. He thought girls were a lot to handle and would rather have all boys. I don't know where he got that idea.

The sonographer called just me in first, as she had done with the previous two pregnancies, and got all the measurements to make sure the baby was healthy. Once she was finished, she called Jimmy and Cody in to reveal the gender. She turned the screen to us and announced, "It's a girl." Cody immediately cried and threw himself on the ground in three-year-old fit fashion, and Jimmy said ever so quietly under his breath, "Oh man." I turned to her with a smile and a shrug and responded, "Well, I'm excited." We all laughed, except for Cody who was distraught over having a sister and was still on the ground. Eventually the boys came around and were excited about a baby girl in the house.

This little girl had already proved to be hard to handle with my sickness in the beginning, but it didn't stop there. Around thirty weeks pregnant, I began to have regular contractions almost daily. Several times I would have to stop working and rest until they resolved. After several trips to the hospital for preterm contractions by thirty-four weeks, my doctor put me on medicine to stop labor and took me off work. I don't rest and sit well, so those next three weeks were torture at home.

At thirty-seven weeks, I finally went into labor that they didn't stop. This delivery was the easiest of all three, thank goodness, because the pregnancy was the worst. I was only in labor for about four hours before she made her debut, barely enough time to get the epidural first. On October 7, 2009, Camille Claire "Millie" made her entrance into the world. She was so pretty and perfect. Immediately she stopped crying when I held her and nursed her with ease. We were in the hospital for less than twenty-four hours before we took her home. I felt less like an emotional basket case this time. I don't know if it was age, feeling more settled, or what, but I just felt happy and content. I thought about Reed often in those first few days, but more in a nostalgic way. I wished I could've experienced all this with him, but I was content with where I was at that moment—physically and emotionally.

Things seemed a little bit easier this time. I guess I was more prepared. I was more prepared for the exhaustion, the constant duties, and the physical recovery. I was also more prepared for the emotions and flashbacks to my first pregnancy with Reed. I didn't linger as long on the negative emotions and thoughts. I knew things were how they were supposed to be at the moment. It just felt right. Don't get me wrong. She didn't sleep well for about five months, unless I was holding her. She wanted to eat all the time, and I was the only one who could feed her. But we all loved her so much, even Cody.

CHAPTER

18

In the fall of 2010, when Cody was four, we planned to take him to his first LSU football game. If you've never been to an LSU football game, you should. It's quite an experience. We had a whole day planned out. We had decided to leave Millie at home because she was still a baby and would not have enjoyed it much. We would tailgate and cook with our friends and their kids, walk around campus, watch the band march into the stadium, and of course go to the game.

Over the past few years, the visits with Tammy, Rickie, and Reed had slowed. Our life with two kids had gotten busier and their lives were as well. I tried not to dwell on it too often, though I thought of them at least once a day. I had spoken to Tammy a few days before the game and we had decided we would meet up. I was so excited to see them and for Cody to meet Reed, who was eleven at the time. I didn't know what to expect, but I can tell you I didn't expect my heart to be so full that day.

We arrived early that morning in our full-out LSU gear. Cody had on football pants, jersey, and helmet. He was pumped. It was nonstop chatter from all the kids, who were all so excited. I could not concentrate much on conversation. I kept checking my phone for Tammy to call and say they were ready to meet up. I couldn't wait for this encounter. We hadn't really said much to Cody, who was four, except that we were going to meet up with some of our friends. He didn't question it. Finally, after a few hours of cooking, eating, and playing football in the grass, Tammy called.

We decided to meet up at the tiger's cage, yet another must-see on an LSU football outing. I could see them standing around the cage as we walked up: Tammy, Rickie, Reed, and Adam (Tammy and Rickie's other son). I sped up my pace a little bit trying to reach them faster. It was always like seeing them the first time every time; my heart always longed for these visits. I hugged each of them when we met up and introduced Cody and Reed. Reed immediately, without hesitation, started playing with Cody. Tammy and I watched in awe as they naturally drew to one another and bonded. They threw the football around and played chase for a while. It was like they had known each other forever. When we headed to go watch the band play, the boys were walking together a few feet in front of Tammy and me. Cody just reached up and grabbed Reed's hand, and they smiled at each other and kept on walking as if that was just the most normal, everyday thing. Tammy grabbed my arm to make sure I saw as I was pulling out my phone to snap a picture. Although I didn't need a photo, that image will forever be etched in my mind.

My heart just about burst. I had been praying for them to have a relationship since Cody had been born, and it was just that simple. I had built it up in my mind to be difficult and messy, and it just wasn't. If we could all trust and love like kids, man, this world would be so much easier. It was the beginning of my realization of all the grace and mercy I had received from God. This beautiful moment came out of such pain for so many years.

We walked to see the band and the boys stuck by each other's side the rest of the time. Cody sat on Reed's shoulders as the band passed and they cheered together. I still just couldn't believe what I was witnessing. I was always afraid of them pulling away from us at some point, but this moment proved that wasn't going to happen; these boys were bonded already. My heart settled for a while. We parted ways when it was time for the game. Reed and Cody hugged goodbye; it was so sweet. I think I floated up to my seat and was in a beautiful fog for the rest of the day.

A few days later, Cody asked me if we could go back to Baton Rouge to see his cousin. I racked my brain trying to think of a cousin who lived there that he had met and was stumped. I said, "Who are you talking about? We don't have any cousins there." He was adamant and said, "Yes, we do. My cousin Reed!" Never had I said anything about Reed being family. He felt that connection on his own in his four-year-old heart. He couldn't wait until the next time we would go see his "cousin" Reed.

We did go back and see his "cousin" Reed, and this time we brought Millie. She was too young to remember or know, but I was happy that we all connected as if one big family. Each time we visited, Cody and Reed would pick right back up as if long-lost friends or cousins.

> Take delight in the Lord, and he will give you the desires of your heart. (Psalm 37:4)

CHAPTER 19

IN THE SPRING OF 2013, MY ADOPTION WORLD WAS SHAKEN FOR the second time. The first time was in 2008 when Tammy was diagnosed with breast cancer. At the time of her initial diagnosis, I was sad, mad, and heartbroken. She assured me that the doctors felt it was very treatable and she would be fine. She went through surgery, chemo, and radiation. My heart ached for Reed having to endure watching his mom go through all the sickness and pain.

The business of my life with school, work, and kids kept me from visiting much during that time. I'm ashamed to admit I didn't want to either. I was in denial that this was happening and was happy to be out of sight and out of mind. I know it wouldn't have changed anything, but I would give anything to go back now and visit more during that time.

When Tammy went into remission, I felt a huge sigh of relief. I thanked God often for healing my child's mother. I felt like God had given us all a second chance to strengthen our relationship and bonds.

I certainly wasn't expecting the bomb she dropped on us in the spring of 2013.

Tammy and Rickie had season LSU baseball tickets and had offered to let us use them to take the kids to a baseball game. We drove the Baton Rouge and met them at a gas station to get the tickets. Tammy got out all smiles and hugged all of us. She said she needed to tell me something, but not today. It could wait. I did not sense anything in her voice to make me think something was wrong. I told her I would call her next week and we could talk. She seemed fine with that and I honestly didn't give it a second thought.

The next week when I called her, I didn't expect the news I got. She told me that her cancer had returned and had spread to several places. What? I quit listening after that. How could this be? God had healed her; she was in remission. Why her? She told me she had already been to MD Anderson and would be starting chemo soon. She seemed very optimistic that she would be OK. I wasn't sure if I believed her this time. I knew the dangers of a cancer recurrence. I wasn't so sure she would be OK this time, and I was not OK with that. I was so angry. I was angry with God. Hadn't he led me to this family and helped me choose them as parents for my child? Then why would he take one of them away from him? A motherless home was not what I signed my child up for. I was distraught and didn't know where to turn.

I bottled up my anger, turned it into bitterness, and held it in. Only my very close friends and family knew what was going on. It wasn't something I wanted to talk about much. I put on a fake smile and went about my days as if everything were fine. There were days this was easier than others, and there were days I would break down and just cry. I would cry for myself and the possible loss of someone I had drawn so close to, and I cried for Reed and how his heart must be breaking. I could not imagine the daily struggles she had and how it affected their family. I just couldn't understand.

I didn't share any of my fears with Tammy, though maybe I should have. She was always so strong. Anytime I saw her during her cancer battle, she put a smile on her face and did her best to appear like everything was going to be OK. I felt myself pull away from them a bit. I didn't want to face the reality of the situation: that she might die. I was terrified of that. Terrified for Reed, Rickie, and Adam, and terrified for myself. So I stopped calling as much, and when I did, I asked how they were doing but just glazed over the cancer stuff. I wanted to ask if it was going away but didn't because I really didn't want the answer.

CHAPTER 20

In the months following Tammy's rediagnosis, I was definitely in a faith slump. While Jimmy and I had been going to church more often at this time, my relationship with God was not at its best. I still didn't find myself worthy enough to get close to him and kept him at arm's length in my life. At a time when it would have been good to draw near to him and lean on my faith, I did not.

In the fall of 2013, Jimmy went on a men's retreat that was put on by our church parish. When he returned, he had this new calm and peace about him and a renewed interest in our faith. He insisted that I go on the next women's retreat so that I could have a chance to experience what he had. I reluctantly agreed. I knew I could use some peace and calm in my life, but I also knew what would happen at this retreat. I had been to enough retreats in high school to know that they would tear down my walls before rebuilding them in faith. It was the tearing down that I was afraid of.

I had spent many years building these steel walls around the guilt and shame surrounding my past and had gotten pretty good at pretending they weren't there. I was afraid to tear them down and expose the wounds. I was afraid to feel it all again. I was afraid to give control over to God. What if I didn't like where he wanted my life to go? I went, despite my hesitation.

From the first day of being there, I felt the calm. I knew that this was where God wanted me at this very moment. I felt that he wanted me to bring all my wounds to him and let him heal my heart. There was not simply one moment of healing. Throughout the weekend, there were women who shared their faith journeys and the struggles they had encountered in their lives. There was one who had adopted, one who was adopted, and many who had just struggled with past shame. I could not believe the coincidence of the similarities in the stories. God has been with them the whole journey, and it made me realize that he had been with me through the years too. This realization came not only from the stories but from lots of little moments like nailing my guilt and shame to the cross, a priest encouraging me to forgive myself and receive God's mercy, a letter from Tammy thanking me for all I had done for her (which still sits in my nightstand), and many others where I felt the love and mercy of God. He didn't erase my past or fix the heartaches, but he showed me in those few days how he had been by my side all along. He showed me that even in my darkest hours, he had lit my path.

Over the next few months after the retreat, I really focused on my family and my faith. I felt like I could face the hardships to come with God by my side and a community to support me. I couldn't control life or death when it came to Tammy, so I had to put her healing in God's hands, whatever that would mean.

I talked with Tammy often during this time and would ask her how she was feeling. She would sometimes avoid answering or change the subject. When she would talk about her treatment, she always remained positive and told me not to worry. I did worry, but probably not as much as I would have before. I knew that God had a plan and would take care of her. The peace I had received at the retreat had carried over into my relationship with Tammy and my fears for Reed's future. I tried not to dwell on those fears and focused on the now.

CHAPTER 21

Cody played travel baseball for several years and we would go to different cities on the weekends for tournaments. Whenever we were playing in Baton Rouge, I would try to get time to meet up with Tammy, Rickie, and the boys. Reed and his brother were getting older and were busy themselves, so it would often just be Tammy.

In the fall of 2014, while we were playing baseball in Baton Rouge, Tammy came to visit at the ballpark. It was the first time in a while that I had seen her. I chose not to acknowledge it at the time, but she looked sick. It was the first time I remember her looking sick. She had a large jacket covering her frail body, a hat covering her bald head, and puffy cheeks from all the medication. She didn't have the same twinkle in her eye, and I could tell she felt bad. She sat and visited anyway. She lied to me and told me her treatments were going well and that she was hopeful for the future. I chose to believe her. My medical brain was blinded by my strong will for her to survive this. She stayed for a while and visited, and even met some of my friends that day. That particular visit is vivid in my memory. I can see us sitting there at the ballpark, amid all the chaos, talking as if it were only us there. Just her presence would put my mind at ease. She had a way to bring optimism to any situation. As always, she told me not to worry about her, that

God was taking care of her. She hugged me when she left that day and told me she loved me.

A few months later, in spring of 2015, we were back headed to Baton Rouge for a tournament. On our way down there, I texted Tammy as I usually did and asked if she wanted to visit. I didn't get a response from her that day, which was unusual. The next day I got a text back from her phone, but it was from Rickie. He explained that Tammy had not been feeling well and was in the hospital getting some fluids and medicine. He wished us luck in our games and said he would call me later in the week to talk. My heart sank. I knew what was coming; she had been sick for a while now. I could hardly think of anything else until I heard from him.

Rickie called me the next week and told me they had decided to take Tammy home on hospice. I didn't know what to say. I asked him how long she had left, and he said not that long, that she was losing strength quickly. I asked if I could come visit her one last time. We agreed I would come one day while the boys were at school that week. I was sad and grateful at the same time. I was so grateful that he was going to let me come see her, but so sad that it would be the last time I would talk to her.

I got off work at 7 a.m. on a Monday in March 2015 and got in a car with my mom. We headed to Baton Rouge to visit Tammy for the last time. Over the years, my mom had come with me many times to visit them and had grown close to Tammy as well. When I told her Tammy wasn't going to be here much longer, she quickly offered to drive me to see her. I stared out the window for most of the ride there, not wanting to talk about what we were about to face. I was silently praying to God to give me the words to say to Tammy and the strength to say goodbye. My heart was breaking.

My mom and I pulled into Tammy and Rickie's driveway and parked the car. Rickie quickly met us outside. He hugged us both and said he was glad we had come. He led us into the house where Tammy's sister was waiting for us in the kitchen. Up until this point, I had not met any of the members of their families. They had kept the other parts of their lives separate from me, and I was nervous to meet her. She looked just like Tammy and was just as inviting as she hugged me. She seemed happy to meet me and that made me relived. I certainly didn't want to cause any trouble. They had enough to deal with already.

We walked over to where Tammy was lying in the living room. She was in a hospital bed near the window. I was taken aback by how small and sick she looked. She didn't look like the Tammy I knew. She was lying there with her eyes closed. Rickie gently woke her up and told her we were there to see her. She looked at me, smiled, and lifted her weak arms to hug me. Tears immediately rolled down my face as I hugged her. She felt so thin, but her hug was just as warm and genuine as it had been on the first day I met her, the day God sent her to save me and my baby.

We all sat down around her bed—I sat in the chair right next to her so that I could hold her hand—and talked for a while. She asked about Jimmy, Cody, and Millie. She asked about work and what I was doing. She told me the latest with the boys and even poked fun at Rickie's hovering over her. We talked like nothing was going on, like this was just a regular visit. It was good, for both of us I think, to just talk and laugh. Rickie and Tammy's sister were in and out of the room, busy with calls and other things, so mostly it was just Tammy, Mom, and me. I could tell Tammy was getting tired after we had been there for a while, but I didn't want to go. I wanted this time to last forever. I knew it would be the last time I saw her and there was so much I needed to say. I asked my mom if I could talk to Tammy alone for a minute before we left. She hugged Tammy and went to join Rickie and Tammy's sister in the kitchen.

Once we were alone, she told me she had asked Reed a few days prior if he wanted her to tell him about his birthparents and he had said no, not right now. I told her I had been wondering if he knew about me. She reassured me that he would in his time and that he would love me as much as she did. She had always sensed my fear and insecurity there and had tried to ease my concerns through the years. Even in her last moments, she was taking care of me.

I scooted my chair closer to her and looked at her with tears rolling down my cheeks. I held her hand and said, "I'm not sure what to say right now. How do I thank you for all you have done for me? Thank you for taking care of Reed when I couldn't." She said, "Oh Tracy, I should be thanking you. You gave me the greatest gift ever. You are so special to me." I told her I would miss her so much and that I would make sure Reed remembered how special she was.

My one regret from that visit is that I didn't ask her to pray with me. I wish I had been bold enough to ask, but I didn't. I know God was there anyway. Hadn't he always been? He had orchestrated our entire relationship, and he wasn't even close to done. Still isn't.

I hugged her one last long time and she told me not to worry. I told her I loved her, and she said she loved me too. I did not want to let go. I wanted to stay in that moment for as long as possible. I knew in my heart it would be the last time I hugged her or talked to her, and I didn't want it to end. I finally gathered the strength to walk away, not wanting to but knowing it was time.

I walked to where my mom and Rickie were talking outside. He hugged me tightly and said he was so glad I had come. I asked him how long she had left, and he responded, "Not long. Maybe days." I asked him to let me know when she passed. He knew Jimmy and I were leaving soon to go to Disney for vacation with the kids, so he told me no. He said he wouldn't let us know if it was while we were on vacation. He said Tammy would not be OK with ruining your family trip. He told me to call him when I got back, and we could talk. I told him I would be praying for all of them and that I was here if they needed. Reed and Adam were at school while we were visiting, so I didn't get a chance to see Reed. I was so worried about him too. I couldn't imagine the pain of losing a parent at the age of sixteen. This had to be so hard for him. I hoped he knew how much she loved him and would be watching over him from heaven. She loved him so much, and I know it was hurting her to leave him. I hoped he knew that he had a birth mother who loved him too and would want to have a relationship one day. I would never *ever* be able to replace Tammy, nor would I try, but I know she would want us to have a relationship. I hoped he would reach out one day and I could be there for him.

After one more hug, Mom and I got into her car to drive back home. It was a very quiet drive. I didn't feel like talking. When she dropped me off at home, I crawled in my bed and didn't get out until the next day. I cried and slept. I didn't want to feel this, and I didn't want to talk to anyone about it. The anger started to build up in me. How could God do this? Was this really happening? My son was losing his mother, and I was losing my lifeline to him. Rickie had always been there, but Tammy was the one I had always leaned on. Would Rickie even want to keep our relationship going? Would he understand what I needed as a mother? I was overcome with fear and doubt. I prayed for God to give me faith, but I just didn't feel it.

I tried to push thoughts of Tammy out of my mind while we were on vacation, but it was difficult. I wondered each day if she was still alive. On the way home, I got word that she had passed the day we had left for our vacation and that her memorial had been the day before we headed home. I had missed it. My children didn't know the details of the adoption or even about it at all, so I couldn't very well let them see me fall apart in the car. I felt like my world had just been shaken and I didn't know what to do. Tears fell down my face as we drove, and Jimmy held my had tightly. I reflected on our journey as mothers to the same child. Visions of all our visits, from the first meeting to saying goodbye, flashed through my mind. We had so many wonderful memories. I thanked God for the time I had gotten to know and love her. I asked him to increase my faith that this would not be the end but the beginning of something new.

Not only did he bring something beautiful out of this, but I did not see coming the beautiful blessings he would bring out of this darkness.

> But though he cause grief, he will have compassion according to the abundance of his steadfast love. (Lamentations 3:32)

CHAPTER

22

The first few months after Tammy's death, I didn't hear from Rickie much. He would text every now and then or I would text to check on him. I was constantly worried about the future of our relationship. Would he continue it like Tammy had? Every time he would text me, I would get butterflies as I opened it, worried he would be texting to say he didn't want any further communication. It never was though. It was always something positive. *Always.* I don't know why I doubted so much. I can see now God had a plan, but my vision was so clouded with worry back then. I was so worried I would lose my line to Reed and knew I wouldn't be able to handle that.

A few months after she passed, Rickie suggested we meet up at one of Reed's cross-country races. He had been running for a few years and we usually tried to make at least one race per year. His state cross-country meet of his junior year was a few weeks away, not far from where we lived, so I said I would come to that one. Cody got wind that I was going and begged me to take him out of school to go. Cody had jumped at the chance to visit Reed any time he could since that LSU game where they had met. They always seemed to pick right up and had acted like brothers, though neither of them knew the truth. I was secretly glad Cody was going with me. This would be the first time I had seen them since Tammy's passing, and

I was nervous to go. On the day of the race, I checked Cody out of school and we headed to Natchitoches, Louisiana.

Any ten-year-old who gets to leave school early is super excited, but Cody was especially talkative that day. It is only about a forty-five-minute drive there, and I think he talked the whole time. He asked lots of questions about Reed too. "How are we related to Reed, Mom?" "If we aren't related, how do we know him?" "How long have you known him, Mom?" "You and his mom were good friends, huh?" I could barely answer one before the next question came. I asked him why he was asking all these questions, all the while dodging the true answers to them. He said, "I don't know. I've just been thinking about it." I danced around the real answers to some of the questions and was able to give real answers to others. I wasn't ready to reveal the truth and hoped he couldn't see through my answers. How long have I known him? His whole life. Was I good friends with his mom? You have no idea. Yes, wonderful friends. He was satisfied with my answers and moved on to talking about something else. I pretended to be engaged in whatever he was talking about, but I could not stop thinking about his questions. Could I tell him the truth? Was he ready to hear it? Was he too young to know?

We arrived at the meet a few minutes later, and I welcomed the distraction. Rickie met us at the gate and walked with us to the starting line. If you've never been a spectator at a cross-country race, it's quite comical. You sprint from one location to the next to cheer for your runner along the course. It's a workout in itself. Cody and I ran with Rickie from one spot to another while cheering on Reed, who was doing very well. All the runners finished on the track in the stadium, so we headed there to watch the finish. Rickie had tears of pride in his eyes as Reed entered the stadium in the top ten. We cheered loudly as he crossed the finish line fourth in the state. After he finished, I saw him look up in the sky and make a gesture that I know was for Tammy. I know he ran with her wings that day, and she was so proud of him. I was proud of him. I was proud that despite all he had been through in the last six months, he still gave it his all. I was proud of the young man he was becoming. I was proud to witness this moment with his dad and hug him with tears in both our eyes. I wished Tammy were there to share in this moment. She would have been beaming with pride.

Cody was jumping up and down, so excited to be there for his friend Reed. Just to watch the admiration Cody had for his big brother, without even knowing he was related to him, was amazing. Cody and I hung around while they announced the winners and took all their pictures. Not only had Reed done well individually, but his team had come in first. It was very exciting. Seeing the pure joy on his face after all he had been through in the past few months was worth it. I was so grateful to Rickie for allowing us to be a part of it.

We were kind of standing off to the side awkwardly with Rickie when I saw Reed look over at us and then whisper something to the girl standing next to him. Then she looked over at us. Something about the way they looked at us made me wonder if he knew who we really were or if he thought we were just weird friends of the family who came around every now and then. My heart began to pound as I wondered what they were whispering about. Could he suspect the truth? Was he going to say something today, in front of everyone, in front of Cody?

After a few minutes, Rickie called him over to talk to us. Cody was grinning from ear to ear like Reed was a celebrity. We hugged him, chatted for a minute, took a picture with him, and then he went back to his friends. After talking with Rickie for a few more minutes, we left to head home.

The ride home was quiet. All the excitement and the talking must have worn Cody out because he slept the whole way home. I had been thinking about his questions on the ride there all day. I texted Jimmy about it while I was there, and we had decided I would tell Cody the truth if he asked again, but he slept so I didn't have the chance. During the silence on the ride home, I thought about what this day had meant. All my fears of being shut out of Reed's life after Tammy's passing were squashed. I realized that Rickie had every intention of not only continuing the relationship but was going to allow me to be a part of the big moments in Reed's life. I was so grateful for that. I also realized that the time for telling my kids the truth was coming. That both scared and excited me. I was scared that they would no longer see me the same, that I wouldn't be perfect in their eyes. But even bigger than that was my excitement for what was to come. I could feel the new chapter of our relationship starting and couldn't wait to see what happened next.

CHAPTER 23

Over the next few months, I talked with Rickie a handful of times. We met briefly around Christmas for me to give him Christmas gifts for the boys. He told me he had something for me too. He pulled out a small box with a cross in it. He said he had it made for me with some of Tammy's hair in it. What a thoughtful gift. I hugged him and thanked him a million times. I was so grateful that he had thought of me. Definitely the best gift I received that year. I didn't see Reed that day. He was busy with school stuff. I told Rickie to tell him happy birthday and Merry Christmas from us, and we parted ways. I wore that cross almost daily, especially when I needed to feel her close to me.

A few months later, in early March 2016, I got a text from Rickie at work that he needed to tell me something. *Always* a stomach drop. I responded, "I'm at work, but what's up?" trying to sound as casual as I could even though I was more nervous than I was trying to appear. He said he had walked into his bedroom and found Reed sitting on his bed reading Tammy's obituary. He asked him if everything was OK. Reed put the obituary down, looked up at Rickie, and asked him to tell him about his birthparents. Ricked said he sat down next to Reed and asked him if he had any idea who it could be. He paused for a second and asked, "Is it Tracy?" When Rickie responded yes, he said Reed's face broke out into a huge smile. He said his next question was "Does that make Cody my brother?" Rickie said, "Yes, and Millie is your sister." He showed him the album I had made while pregnant with pictures of me and my family. Ricked said he asked lots of questions and even asked if he could keep some of the pictures.

I was a blubbering mess of joyful tears by the time I finished reading all of Rickie's texts describing the interaction. I was finding it hard to keep my composure while working. I would dry my eyes, see a patient, and then read the texts again. I couldn't believe the moment I had been anticipating since handing over that precious baby had happened. I wish I could have seen his face. Was he happy, relieved, nervous, or fearful? I don't know. I was just so glad it had happened. Rickie felt like Reed may have put something on social media about it, but he wasn't sure. I was just speechless. Not only was he wanting to know about me, but he wanted to share that information with everyone.

While I was getting all these texts from Rickie, I was screenshotting them and sending them to Jimmy and my friend. No one at work knew my story, so I couldn't share with them and I wanted to share with someone. They were both so excited and I was crying all over again. My friend started looking all over Facebook and Instagram for what he could have posted and found it. She took a screenshot and sent it to me. He posted a picture of him and me on his first birthday when I went to his house. He wrote a very sweet message thanking me for giving him life. My heart could hardly handle the happiness. For more than seventeen years, I had been worried about how he would take the news of me. I worried he would be angry or not want anything to do with me. Not only was he not angry with me, but he seemed to be excited about it all. I was honestly shocked it had gone so smoothly. Once again God had come through. I don't know why I didn't trust him to work it all out. He shows up every time and makes things better than I ever dreamed.

While I was relieved that the part of telling Reed was over, it did make it real. Real in the sense that I would have to tell my kids soon. Real in the sense that the next time I saw Reed, he would know who I really was to him: his birth mother. I didn't know when that interaction would be, but I was already a nervous wreck about it.

CHAPTER 24

Rickie and I texted often in the months following Reed's discovery, but it would be several months before I saw them. I knew I wanted to see him since he now knew who I really was. I wanted to see his face. I felt like I would really know how he felt about everything once I could see him face-to-face. What would I say? What would he say?

We made plans to see each other in October 2016 when Reed's cross-country team would be racing near us. I knew I needed to tell my kids the truth of who Reed was before that day, but I had no idea how to do that. How do you tell your children that you've made huge mistakes and that there was a whole life before them? I don't need my kids to think I am perfect, but I sure wasn't prepared to tell them all this. I had always known this day would come eventually, but now that it was here, I had no idea how to do it. I had several people in my life at the time praying for us and praying for me to find the right words. As in many things in my life, it seemed God had other plans for how they were to find out.

One day in late September—yes, I still hadn't told the kids—Millie and I were riding home in the car alone. She was a curious and chatty child so she was always talking about something. This particular day, she was jumping from topic to topic, and I honestly zoned out for a bit and wasn't really paying attention to her. She said something about brothers or sisters and secrets that stopped me in my tracks. I said, "What did you just say?" She responded, "I just feel like I have a brother or a sister that's a teenager that you've been hiding from me all my life." *I'm sorry. What?* I tried to keep my voice as calm as possible. Thank goodness she was sitting behind me and couldn't see the shock on my face. I asked, "What makes you think that?" She said, "I don't know. I just feel it." I blew her off and gave her some blanket response like "Oh Millie, you're so silly."

I guess God grew tired of waiting for me to do it and told Millie himself. I could not believe it. What had just happened? I had been stressing and worrying for months now and here my six-year-old daughter just made it seem like casual conversation. Jimmy and I talked and prayed about it and decided to tell the kids together that Sunday after Mass. I was on pins and needles the whole week. I could barely hold it together during Mass. My biggest secret was about to come out to the people I loved most. How would they react? Jimmy held my hand tight that day and I know he could sense my tension. My friend hugged me after Mass and told me, "God's got this. You just have to say it." She was so right. I got the message from him loud and clear through Millie, and I knew this was what I needed to do.

When we got home from church, we went into our normal routine. I sent the kids to change and bring me their laundry as we usually did. Instead of changing and starting to sort the laundry, I gathered the things I wanted to have for our conversation. I had the photo album that Tammy and Rickie had made for me and an album I had made of pictures from Reed's birth and the days that followed. As I looked through the pictures and tried to gather my thoughts, doubt crept in. Could I do this? What would they think of me after I told them? Maybe they were too young to know the truth.

When the kids walked into my room with their laundry, they were surprised to see me sitting on the floor waiting for them. Jimmy sat next to me and asked the kids to sit down, saying that we needed to talk to them. They sat down and I could tell they were confused.

I started with telling Cody what Millie had said in the car. He laughed and gave Millie a little nudge as if to say, "Yeah, right, like that's possible." I said, "Well, it is true. You have a brother who is seventeen. I had him when I was eighteen and another family adopted him."

They were both speechless. I asked, "Do you have any idea who it could be?" They both paused and were thinking about that when Cody looked at me with excitement in his eyes and asked, "Is it Reed?" When I said yes, he let out a loud cheer and they both had huge smiles on their faces. I thought, *Wow, this was so easy.*

They both had lots of questions but were thrilled to know they had a brother. Without getting into any nitty-gritty details, I answered questions like "Is Daddy his dad?" "Then where is your other husband?" "Why doesn't he live with us?" and most importantly to them, "When can we see him?" I told them we would see him in two weeks when he came for a race. They were beyond excited and started counting the days.

I was so relieved that this had gone so well. I really couldn't believe it. I had analyzed it and worried about it until I was making it complicated. God swooped in and made it a breeze. He started the conversation and gave me the words to say. I was so grateful to have such a huge weight finally lifted.

Now I just had to wait until the day of the meeting. I felt like I had been waiting for this day for my whole life. I guess I had been waiting almost half of my life. Those two weeks felt like years though. I went through every scenario in my mind of what could happen. I tried to focus on the good that could come of it, but my mind always crept to doubt. Maybe he wouldn't want to see us. Maybe he would change his mind. I tried to push those thoughts out of my mind and focus on just taking the next step. That was all I could control anyway. Show up, and God would take it from there, right?

> Fear not, for I am with you, be not dismayed, for I am your God; I will strengthen you, I will help you, I will uphold you with my victorious right hand. (Isaiah 41:10)

CHAPTER 25

ON THE DAY OF THE SCHEDULED RACE WHERE WE WOULD MEET up, I woke up early. I couldn't sleep because I was so excited and nervous. I think the kids were just as excited because they jumped out of bed early on a Saturday when I woke them up. Everyone was ready in record time.

We all piled in the car and drove the twenty minutes to the race. The kids talked the whole way there, asking questions about how the day was going to go and if Reed knew we were coming. I told them all I knew was that we were meeting up after he ran, and we would just see how the day went. I planned to text Rickie when we got there but didn't think we would see them until after the race. I kind of hoped we wouldn't see them until after the race. I needed more time to gather myself and my thoughts. What was I going to say when I saw him? What would he say? My thoughts were going a mile a minute.

We parked and walked over to where the finish line would be. My niece was also running in the race so we went to stand with my sister-in-law and brother-in-law. They knew what was happening that day and hugged me and asked what the plan was. I shrugged and said I don't really know; I was just taking it as it came. I texted Rickie to let him know we made it and that we would see him after the race. He quickly responded, "Where are you?" I told him we were at the finish line, and he said, "OK. We are coming to you."

Now? Really? OK. I'm not ready. Hold on. Wait. Really?

My heart started to race. I told Jimmy they were coming now. We had told the kids we wouldn't see them until after the race so they had already run off to play. I nervously scanned the crowd for them. I saw Rickie first, and when our eyes met, he smiled and waved. I waved back. Then I saw that Reed was walking with him. I couldn't even look. I was so incredibly nervous. All these years of waiting and wondering when this day would come had arrived. All the previous visits when he didn't know who I really was rushed through my mind. I flashed to the day I handed him over to Tammy and Rickie and immediately ached for her presence. Jimmy, as always, was my rock by my side. He squeezed my hand and gave me a wink as they made their way to us. Just his presence next to me gave me the strength and courage I needed. He had been through this with me almost from the beginning and was just as excited that we were finally taking this step.

No words were spoken as he walked straight up to me and put his arms around me. Tears started pouring down my face as I realized the moment I had been waiting for was here. All the years of fear, worry, and anxiety culminated in this moment of pure relief and joy. I could feel him crying too as we just hugged for what felt like minutes. I am so grateful for my friend who was close by and snapped a picture of that moment. In the picture, you see our warm embrace as well as Rickie looking on with a smile on his face. There was a glow about us that I know was Tammy's presence. I could feel her there and her approval of all this. I wished she could have been there to witness it and be a part of it, but that just wasn't God's plan. I know this moment had been orchestrated by him. Never in my wildest dreams did I think it would turn out this way and be so easy. That could only have come from God.

I wanted to stay in that moment. It was hard to let him go, but I did and we both dried our tears. He kept saying thank-you over and over. It was overwhelming. Thank me? No, *thank you.* Thank you for wanting to meet and accepting all that had happened. I hugged Rickie and we chatted briefly before Reed had to go prepare for the race. The kids were still off with their friends, unaware that Reed had come over. They could see him after the race. This was my time.

As we watched his race in our usual run around the course fashion, I could not stop smiling. This all felt so surreal. Cody and Millie cheered him on at each turn and were so excited when he crossed the finish line. He walked straight up to me after the race, crying, and hugged me again. We both cried as he thanked me over and over again for everything and for coming. I told him there was nowhere else I would rather be, and I meant it. After all, I had been waiting for this day for years.

Cody and Millie had been as patient as they could while waiting for their turn to hug Reed. I'm not sure who was more excited in that moment: Reed or Cody and Millie. They all hugged. The light in all their eyes was a sight to see. It was as if they had known each other for years. Rickie made his way over to us and we started talking. Reed took that moment to hang with Cody a bit by themselves. He took Cody back to his team tent to meet his friends and hang out. I have the sweetest picture of them walking away together that day, Cody's face looking toward Reed with such admiration. It was as if no one even missed a beat. He was their brother and that was that. There was no turning back now.

CHAPTER

26

I STILL DIDN'T QUITE KNOW MY PLACE. WELL, IF I'M HONEST, I still don't. Was that it? Would he want to see us more? I wasn't sure. I texted with Rickie over the next months periodically. I wasn't brave enough to ask for Reed's number yet, and I wasn't sure how he would feel about me having it. I was in this limbo kind of place where I was excited that we had taken the next step but wasn't sure which step to take after that. I wish I had had someone to talk to about it back then—someone who had gone through something similar.

Cody, my mom, and I decided to go to Reed's state meet that year. My mom was so excited for this next chapter. She was asking all the time if I had talked to Rickie again, when was I going to see Reed, and if could she come. It was a little overwhelming at times. I wasn't sure where I stood with Reed and I didn't want my mom to crowd him too. I asked Rickie if it was OK to bring my mom, and he quickly said sure. We did our usual running around during the race, cheering Reed on at every turn. When we went into the stadium for the finish, Rickie's parents were waiting in the bleachers. I wondered how they would react to us. I didn't have to wonder for long. His mother jumped up and hugged all three of us and told us she was so excited to meet us. They were exactly what you would picture when you picture grandparents. She talked to Cody and told him to call her Grandma. It was so sweet. They just welcomed us as part of the family with no hesitation. Yet another moment that I had made out to be difficult in my mind that just wasn't. After the race, she hugged us goodbye and told us she loved us. Melted my heart. I could feel her genuineness in her hug. She meant it. I was so glad to be accepted in his family too.

We talked to Reed after the race, but only for a minute. He had to get back to his team and they had not won so his spirits were low. Despite that, he hugged us all and thanked us for coming. He was so genuine. It did me good to see him and talk to him, to see that he still wanted to be a part of our lives. I had wondered if the first meeting had been a dream. Was it real? Seeing him and hugging him again made it real.

The next month had his birthday, and I really wanted to call him on that day. I had always called Tammy or Rickie on that day, but this year I wanted to call him. I got up the nerve to ask Rickie for Reed's number. I gathered the kids on his birthday, and we FaceTimed him to sing to him. He smiled the whole time. It was amazing. I wondered how in the world I had gotten here. I was calling my son on his eighteenth birthday for the first time ever. It was short but perfect.

After that, the floodgates had been opened. We started texting every now and then. I kept him updated on the kids' activity schedules, and he kept me informed of his. We went to a couple of his track meets to watch him race in Baton Rouge. He kept promising Cody he would come to one of his basketball or baseball games. One weekend in the spring, he texted that he could come for the day on a Saturday. Really! A whole day here with us. Oh my goodness, we were all excited.

He came over after lunch on a Saturday. Cody's game wasn't until seven, so we had lots of time to hang out. He and the kids mostly played outside while Jimmy and I sat in chairs and watched. While I was sitting there, I felt this cool breeze and looked up at the clouds. I just felt at peace. I felt her: Tammy. I knew this would have made her so happy. I know she would have sat right there beside us, enjoying the weather and watching the kids play. It just felt right.

At the basketball game, Reed may have gotten a bit bombarded. Most of my friends knew of him but had never met him and a few were at the game. He seemed happy to see what our life and friends were like. I'm sure he had been curious. He cheered on Cody and gave him some pointers after the game. We had plans to go to my parents' house after the game for dinner. I didn't think he would want to go, but he did. I was so excited. A few of my dad's siblings were in town and they were happy to finally meet him. He just joined right in and fit in. It was great. Everyone welcomed him with open arms. My grandmother wrapped him in a big hug and gave him a kiss on the cheek. Each step in this new journey brought more peace to my heart. I felt accepted because he was accepted. I was so grateful that it had gone so well.

When we got home, I thought he would need to head home, but he stayed a little longer. Jimmy and I put the kids to bed and Jimmy slipped off to bed to give us some alone time. We stayed up talking until 1 a.m. I don't even know what we talked about. It just felt normal. I had been so worried that things would be weird and awkward, but they really weren't. It was easy. He just fit with us. I had always tried not to play the what-if game with my thoughts, but I couldn't help it that night. What if things had been different? What if he had grown up here with us? Would it have been the same? I know the answer was no. Both our lives would have looked very different if that had been the case. And who knows if this is where we would have ended up? I had to just look forward and trust that this was the way it was intended to be.

CHAPTER 27

For months I had known when Reed's graduation would be. I had asked Rickie for the date back in the fall. I had made sure I was off the day before and the day after just in case we were invited. The weeks leading up to it, we went to his graduation party at his house. We talked about the day. A graduation announcement came in the mail, but no invitation. I was starting to come to the realization that I was not going to get to go, when the text from Reed came. "Would you like to come to my graduation?" I would love to! He said all four of us could come. I knew it was invitation only and he had a certain number of seats he could invite. I made sure he had room for all of us, and he assured me we could all come. The kids were a little excited.

On the day of graduation, we arrived at the convention center where it would be held and waited for Rickie in the lobby for the tickets. He smiled when he saw us and waved us over to the group he was standing with. As we walked up, I realized that this must be their family. I saw Tammy's sister, who I had already met, and hugged her to say hello. There were others I had not met, and Rickie quickly introduced us. Tammy's family was there. I wasn't sure if this was supposed to be awkward or not. I tried to stand to the side so as not to make them feel uncomfortable. Rickie started handing out tickets, and I noticed there were two colors. He handed Jimmy,

Cody, and Millie one color and me a different color. I asked him why mine was different and he smiled and said, "You're sitting with me." It was time to sit, so no time to dwell on the fact that I would not be sitting with Jimmy and the kids. I followed Rickie, Adam, Tammy's sister, and maybe others, to our seats as Jimmy and the kids followed the rest.

When we got to our seats, which were near the front, I tried to scoot in the middle so that the others could sit on the end and Rickie stopped me. He said, "No, you're sitting right by me." I did what he said and sat down. It took me a minute to realize what was happening. I was in her seat. I was in Tammy's seat. I got so overwhelmed I almost cried, but I held it in. So many times over the past few months I had felt her presence and her approval, and here I was in her spot. I would have given anything to let her have that spot. I know she would have been so proud of Reed that day. But I was so thankful that Rickie felt I should sit there. I felt so loved and included.

The graduation ceremony was beautiful. I tried not to let my thoughts distract me from being in the moment. I was so proud of the man Reed was becoming. I knew he had overcome so much heartache and was still shining. When they filed out of the room, he walked right by us and smiled so genuinely when he saw me. Just when I thought my heart was full, it overflowed. After graduation, Rickie invited us to have lunch with the family. I was unsure if that was the right thing to do. I didn't want to intrude, but he insisted.

The large table of all of their family was a little overwhelming. I wasn't sure how they all felt about Reed and my relationship and if they would be upset with us for being there. The kids fought over who got to sit by him and eventually ended up on either side of him, monopolizing him for the meal. Tammy's family asked Jimmy and me some questions and were very polite and friendly. I felt they were unsure about us but gave us a chance anyway.

We sat there for a long time just talking before it was time to go. When we stood up to leave, each of Tammy's siblings and her mother hugged me and told me thank-you over and over. I tried to tell them through my tears how much I loved and missed Tammy and that she had been so good to me. Tammy's mom hugged me tightly and said, "Thank you for giving us the gift of Reed." I was so overcome with gratitude for them. I could not believe how wonderful they were to me, just like Tammy. I guess that's where she got it from.

We said our goodbyes to everyone and to Reed and headed home. I was so thankful to God for that day. It was even better than I could have hoped for.

> These things I have spoken to you, that my joy may be in you, and that your joy may be full. (John 15:11)

Now

It's been twenty-three years since I stared at that stick on the back of the toilet, twenty-two years since Reed made his entry into my life and changed it forever, six years since Tammy left us, four years since that graduation day, one week since Reed spent the weekend with us, and thirty minutes since my last conversation with Reed. That conversation was him calling me to wish me a happy Mother's Day twenty-three years after I found out I was going to be a mom. Never in my wildest dreams did I think things would turn out like they have. He truly has become a part of our family. He calls and visits often. Sometimes I hear Cody on the phone late at night, and when I ask him who he's talking to, it's always Reed. They have a bond that I always hoped they would. He has come with us on summer vacations with my parents and has bonded with many of our close friends.

God has blessed me, and my family, more than I thought I deserved. I honestly spent a lot of time thinking I didn't deserve the blessing I was being given. What I have learned though is that God's love and mercy are truly limitless. Literally the sky is the limit. He has loved me and carried me through this journey. Even in those very dark days, he was there. I didn't feel him, but he was there guiding me along the path to where we are today. I know he is not finished with my story and I am learning to trust where he is leading me, like writing this book, a journey that has taken a few years and lots of tears. I wouldn't say he has completely healed my heart through this writing, but he has definitely helped me put more pieces back together through it.

On to the next step of the journey, whatever that will mean! Jesus, I trust in you.

Acknowledgments

Thank you first and foremost to God for guiding me, leading me, inspiring me, and giving me the courage to write all this down. He has been steadfast in his love for me, even when I didn't feel it or see it. I can't give him enough praise and thanks for all he has done in my life.

Thank you to my sweet husband, Jimmy, who has been by my side since the beginning of this journey. When I doubted, he didn't. When I stumbled, he picked me up. Thank you for your love and encouragement through all this writing process, and so much more.

Thank you to my kids, Reed, Cody, and Millie. You are the sweetest and most supportive people I could ask for. I can't believe God has entrusted you to me. I can't wait to see what he has in store for you too.

Thank you to my great friend Holly. You have listened, encouraged, pushed, and loved me these past years. I thank you for your friendship. I thank you for the many hours you spent reading, editing, and making me continue to go deeper. I am so thankful for the gift of you in my life.

Thank you to my many friends and prayer warriors—you know who you are—who have held me up through this process. Your prayers mean more than you will ever know. Thank you to those friends who read, edited, and sometimes told me like I needed to hear it.

Thank you to my parents, who didn't know I was even doing this until it was finished. Your love for me and my family is felt every day. I can't begin to repay you for all the things you have done for me.

Thank you to Rickie and Tammy for sharing your life with me. Thank you for allowing me to be a part of your story. Thank you for always treating me like family.